EVERYDAY HANDBOOKS

IMPROVING YOUR
CHESS

excerpted from the
SECOND, THIRD, FOURTH and *FIFTH*
BOOKS OF CHESS, and *1001 BRILLIANT*
CHESS SACRIFICES AND COMBINATIONS
by Fred Reinfeld

by **FRED REINFELD**

BARNES & NOBLE BOOKS

A DIVISION OF HARPER & ROW, PUBLISHERS

New York, Evanston, San Francisco, London

TABLE OF CONTENTS

IMPROVING YOUR
CHESS

1. BEFORE YOU BEGIN

As a CHESSPLAYER, you lose games from time to time—like all chessplayers.

Naturally you want to improve your play. Is there something special or unique about your problem? I don't think so. Only a few of us can become masters; yet the rest of us can achieve respectable playing strength with a reasonable amount of application.

The first big step—an enormous step—in improving our play is to become aware of the things we do wrong, the bad moves we make. Many of us could never reach that point without personal lessons because we could not previously find in books the kind of material that would enable us to spot our own weaknesses.

That is a pity, for while chess is a lot of fun, win or lose, it's more fun when you win! In my contacts with thousands of chessplayers for over twenty years, I have often watched them grope and drift and become discouraged in their efforts to improve their game.

It was from these observations that the notion of concentrating on the Eight Bad Moves took shape. Again and again I have seen, in the course of teaching and playing and discussing, that most players commit certain *typical* errors.

I started to think about these errors and how to describe them in such a way that the reader would exclaim, "At last! That's just why my games go wrong! If only I'd realized this sooner!"

This book has been "on my mind" for several years. What held me back somewhat in writing it, was the influence of the teachers and psychologists who have been insisting that a "negative" approach is all wrong. I finally concluded that my emphasis on the Eight Bad Moves was not really negative at all. Before a player can begin to improve, he must clear away the faults that have been spoiling his games and depriving him of well-earned victories.

In your study of these games and ideas you will not only discover the Eight Bad Moves and how to overcome the faults that produce them, you will also encounter a wealth of new ideas and techniques which you will enjoy using in your own games.

To derive the maximum value from this book, there are two features which you will very likely want to review quickly. One is to check up on the relative values of the chessmen. Expressed in points, their values are as follows:

Queen	9 points
Rook	5 points
Bishop	3 points
Knight	3 points
Pawn	1 point

It is important to be absolutely certain of these values, for most games are decided by superiority in force.

Bishops (3 points) and Knights (3 points) are equal in value, but experienced players try to capture a Bishop in return for a Knight.

A Bishop or Knight (3 points) is worth about three Pawns (3 points). If you give up a Knight and get three Pawns in return, you may consider it as more or less an even exchange. If you lose a Knight (3 points) for only a Pawn (1 point), you have lost material and should lose the game, if you are playing against an expert.

If you capture a Rook (5 points) for a Bishop or Knight (3 points), you are said to have "won the Exchange." If you lose a Rook (5 points) for a Bishop or Knight (3 points), you have "lost the Exchange." The other important feature in reading a chess book is to be familiar with chess notation. If you can count up to 8, this presents no problem. You may have heard scare stories to the effect that chess notation is inordinately difficult. This difficulty of chess notation is a myth, circulated by people too lazy to discover how simple and logical it really is.

The following diagram shows you all you need to know about chess notation:

BLACK

QR8	QN8	QB8	Q8	K8	KB8	KN8	KR8
QR7	QN7	QB7	Q7	K7	KB7	KN7	KR7
QR6	QN6	QB6	Q6	K6	KB6	KN6	KR6
QR5	QN5	QB5	Q5	K5	KB5	KN5	KR5
QR4	QN4	QB4	Q4	K4	KB4	KN4	KR4
QR3	QN3	QB3	Q3	K3	KB3	KN3	KR3
QR2	QN2	QB2	Q2	K2	KB2	KN2	KR2
QR1	QN1	QB1	Q1	K1	KB1	KN1	KR1

WHITE

As you see, the squares are *numbered* from both sides of the board; White's KR1, for example, is Black's KR8. Each square is also *named* for the piece occupying the file. (See page 172.)

I honestly believe that *ten minutes' study* of this board is all you need to enable you to play over the games and examples in this book.* Although the compact treatment of games and examples makes only slight demands on your knowledge of chess notation, I should like to advise you to master the notation thoroughly; it will open the gates to a lifetime of reading pleasure.

The following are the chief abbreviations used in the chess notation:

King	— K	discovered check	— dis ch
Queen	— Q	double check	— dbl ch
Rook	— R	en passant	— e.p.
Bishop	— B	castles, king-side	— O—O
Knight	— N	castles, queen-side	— O—O—O
Pawn	— P	good move	— !
captures	— x	very good move	— ! !
to	— —	outstanding move	— ! ! !
check	— ch	bad move	— ?

Here are some examples of abbreviation: N—KB3 means "Knight moves to King Bishop three." Q x B means "Queen takes Bishop." R—K8 ch means "Rook moves to King eight giving check."

---

* If you feel that you need more schooling in learning the notation, almost any primer will be of help. *First Book of Chess* (Barnes & Noble, Inc.: New York, 1952) by Horowitz and Reinfeld, contains an unusually detailed treatment of chess notation.

2. THE EIGHT BAD MOVES

Neglecting Development
of Your Pieces

IN THE ORIGINAL starting position of a game of chess, the pieces are not ready for action. The process by which we advance them to squares on which they can attack and defend and maneuver freely is called "development."

If we develop the pieces slowly or ineffectively, their action is limited. Their attacking ability is slight, and the initiative passes into the hands of our opponent.

If we move one piece repeatedly, it follows that other pieces are being neglected, still left on their original squares where they accomplish nothing. Lagging or ineffective development accounts for many a stinging defeat on the chessboard.

While each opening presents its special problems, there are some practical rules that are helpful guides. Always start by playing out a center Pawn, as this creates a line for developing a Bishop. Bring out the King Knight very early—preferably to KB3. By playing out the King Knight and King Bishop quickly, you make early castling possible and thus get your King out of any immediate danger.

Try to avoid placing your Bishops on diagonals where they are blocked by your own Pawns. Avoid, too, an excessive number of Pawn moves—they contribute little or nothing to development.

Play over your games to see whether you are achieving the following minimum in the first ten moves: both center Pawns advanced; both Knights developed; both Bishops developed; castling completed. This is an ideal goal which you may not always achieve, but it will help you to guard against moving the same piece repeatedly.

Managing the Queen is a different matter. If you develop her too soon you will only expose her to harrying by enemy pieces of lesser value. A later chapter will treat this point in detail.

Disastrous Pawn Moves

KING'S KNIGHT'S OPENING

WHITE	BLACK		WHITE	BLACK
1 P—K4	P—K4		2 N—KB3	N—QB3
	3 B—B4	P—B3??		

Black's 3rd move should have been *3 . . . B—B4 or 3 . . . N—B3*—useful developing moves that prepare for castling.

Instead, the move actually played, 3 . . . P—B3??, is damaging in a number of ways. It is basically bad because it opens up a line of attack on the Black King. (The further play will illustrate the dangers involved.)

Secondly, 3 . . . P—B3?? has the great defect of making it very difficult for Black to castle. The Pawn move extends the diagonal of White's Bishop at QB4 so that the Bishop controls KN8—the square the Black King would occupy in castling.

There might be some point to 3 . . . P—B3?? if the move had good qualities to set off its defects. But it not only has no advantageous features—it even has a fourth defect!—it deprives the Black King Knight of its best square at KB3.

4 N—R4   . . . .

White wants to exploit 3 . . . P—B3?? by playing Q—R5ch.

4 . . . .   P—KN4???

Suicide. Now White's Queen check will lead to checkmate.

5 Q—R5ch   K—K2   6 N—B5 mate

Of the five moves that Black made, three were Pawn moves and one a King move. Aside from contributing nothing to the development of his pieces, the Pawn moves were definitely harmful in opening the gates to the enemy.

Exposing Your King to Attack

THE KING is unlike any other piece. In every game of chess, the object, direct or potential, is to checkmate your opponent's King. No matter how the game proceeds, no matter what your plans may be, you must guard your King and look for opportunities to menace your opponent's King.

Since the King's safety controls the fate of the game, you take unnecessary risks whenever you expose your King to attack. One of the most common ways to endanger the King is to leave him on his original square in the middle of the back rank. The other chess pieces are most active in the center and exert their greatest power in that area. Consequently, the King is most vulnerable at his original square.

Leaving the King in the center is particularly dangerous in "open" positions—those in which there are open files. Such open lines are highways along which the Queen and Rooks can operate to menace the hostile King. (In "closed" position—those in which the Pawn position is locked—a King *may* be fairly safe in the center.)

Leaving the King in the center sometimes leads to ferocious "King-hunts." In the course of such a savage drive on a hostile King, he may be hounded all the way from his original square to the other side of the board. The King-hunt is the extreme example of the helplessness of a King stranded in the center and exposed to the fury of the hostile pieces.

2

WHITE TO MOVE

Here is a good example of the dangers confronting a King in the center in an open position. After 1 QxPch!! Black resigns, for if 1 . . . NxQ; 2 BxP mate.

Knowing that it is bad policy to leave the King exposed to attack in the center, how are we to avoid such dangers? The safest course is to castle fairly early in the game—say no later than the tenth move. Once the King is castled on one side or the other, he is much less vulnerable than in the center.

GIUOCO PIANO

WHITE	BLACK		WHITE	BLACK
1 P—K4	P—K4		4 P—B3	B—N3
2 N—KB3	N—QB3		5 P—Q4	Q—K2
3 B—B4	B—B4		6 P—Q5	....

A questionable move; it closes the diagonal of White's Bishop at QB4 and opens the diagonal of Black's Bishop at QN3.

6 ....   N—Q1

This is a good point for White to castle his King into safety.

7 B—K2?   ....

Incomprehensible. Not only does White neglect to castle; he loses time by moving the already developed Bishop.

| 7 .... | P—Q3 | | 8 P—KR3? | .... |

Again neglecting castling and again wasting time; besides, the Pawn move may turn out to have a weakening effect on White's position.

| 8 .... | P—KB4 | | 10 QN—Q2 | Castles |
| 9 B—KN5 | N—KB3 | | 11 N—R4? | .... |

Once more he misses castling, and once more he fritters away precious time by moving an already developed piece.

| 11 .... | PxP | | 12 NxP | .... |

Calmly relying on the pin on Black's King Knight. But White's numerous violations of chess theory allow Black to violate chess theory too! Black now sacrifices his Queen for a piece of considerably lesser value.

$$12 \ldots\ldots \quad\quad NxN!!$$

3

13 BxQ	BxBPch		14 K—B1 N—N6 mate

What are the technical factors that made this mate possible? First, 7 B—K2? deprived the King of a possible flight square. Secondly, 8 P—KR3? weakened the King-side (allowing the eventual . . . N—N6 mate). Finally, 11 N—R4? resulted in the complete opening of the King Bishop file.

Thus we see that Black's brilliancy was grounded in the shortcomings of White's faulty play. Yet the crowning mistake was White's *failure to castle.*

Making Too Many Queen
Moves in the Opening

REPEATED MOVES with the same piece in the opening are a form of neglected development. While the same piece is moving again and again, the other pieces remain undeveloped. Always a serious fault, it becomes even more serious when the Queen is the piece which is being moved repeatedly. There are a number of reasons for this.

The Queen is by far the strongest piece on the board. It is the heart and soul of a well-managed attack which is based on systematic, *completed* development. To move this powerful piece aimlessly and repeatedly dissipates the attacking power of your position. To move the Queen very early while concentrating on a definite but minor goal, is still bad policy; often much more important features are neglected during these short-sighted maneuvers.

Still another drawback to early Queen moves is that they readily expose the Queen to attack by enemy pieces. So we have here the painful paradox that while one player ignores his development with repeated Queen moves, his opponent develops one piece after another with gain of time by simultaneously attacking the Queen!

Your best course, then, is to follow the advice given on page 5: concentrate on playing out the minor pieces at the beginning of the game; make sure of castling into safety;

and develop the Queen only after the opening development has begun to take shape.

Black Loses Precious Time

KING'S KNIGHT'S OPENING

WHITE	BLACK		WHITE	BLACK
1 P—K4	P—K4		2 N—KB3	Q—B3?

A thoughtless move. Why use the Queen—the most powerful piece on the board—for such menial work as guarding a Pawn?

(*2 . . . N—QB3* performs the same task much more economically.)

3 B—B4   Q—N3?

A second move with the unfortunate Queen.

4 Castles!   QxKP??

And now a third move with the unfortunate Queen. Far ahead in development, White is now ready to exploit the Queen's exposed position.

5 BxPch!   . . . .

For if 5 . . . K x B; 6 N—N5ch forking King and Queen.

5 . . . .   K—K2

5 . . . K—Q1 is slightly better, but the damage is done: Black's King is stranded in the center and has lost the castling privilege.

6 R—K1!   Q—KB5

With a mating attack in the offing, White does not mind sacrificing his Bishop:

7 RxPch!   . . . .

7 . . . .   KxB   8 P—Q4!   . . . .

Gaining valuable time by again attacking the unfortunate Queen.

8 . . . .   Q—B3   11 P—KN4ch!   KxP
9 N—N5ch   K—N3   12 Q—KR3 mate
10 Q—Q3ch   K—R4

An extraordinary game: out of 11 moves, Black made five with his Queen, five with his King. Small wonder that his King was battered into an early checkmate.

Four Consecutive Queen Moves—and "Resigns"

CARO-KANN DEFENSE

WHITE	BLACK	WHITE	BLACK
1 P—K4	P—QB3	3 PxP	PxP
2 P—Q4	P—Q4	4 P—QB4	B—B4

It is poor policy for Black to expose his Queen to immediate attack.

5 PxP	QxP	6 N—QB3	Q—R4
	7 Q—N3	Q—N3	

Still another Queen move.

          8 N—Q5!   ....

If Black now tries to defend the Queen Knight Pawn with *8 . . . Q—QB3*, then the pinning move *9 B—QN5* wins the Queen.

8	QxQ	9 PxQ	Resigns!

Black cannot meet the double threat of 10 N—B7ch or 10 N—N6, winning the Exchange. If he tries *9 . . . N—R3* then *10 RxN!, PxR; 11 N—B7ch* wins for White.

The excessive number of Queen moves has resulted in an undeveloped position lacking adequate defensive resources.

Weakening Your Castled Position

IT STANDS TO REASON that leaving the King in the center often means exposing the King to a dangerous, very possibly fatal, attack. This leads us to the conclusion that castling is the best way to safeguard the King.

The castled position, then, is the King's safeguard. But, though the King is better protected when castled than when in the center, that does not mean that castling alone assures you complete immunity from attack. If your opponent has an overwhelmingly superior development, he can concentrate more forces for attack than you can supply for defense. Sometimes brilliant sacrifices are made to smash down a defender's barriers.

But we are now concerned mainly with *Pawn weaknesses* in the castled position. In the case of castling on the King-side, three Pawns are involved: the King Rook Pawn, the King Knight Pawn, and the King Bishop Pawn. As long as all three Pawns are still on their original squares, the castled position remains strong and difficult to take by storm.

Yet once a single member of the trio advances, the defender is headed for trouble. For example, suppose the King Knight Pawn advances one square. Then immediately the squares it formerly protected—KR3 and KB3—must receive protection from *pieces*. Worse yet, these squares become targets for enemy occupation. Let a hostile Queen and Knight, or Queen and Bishop, occupy these squares, and you will see the castled position totter and crumble.

The advance of the King Rook Pawn is also dangerously weakening. Very often the attacker is able to sacrifice a piece for the Pawn on KR3, in this way ripping up the castled position and leaving it wide open for large-scale invasion. The advance of the King Bishop Pawn creates similar problems, and very often opens up a vital diagonal for the hostile Bishop.

Another serious consequence of any of these Pawn advances is that they enable the attacker to open lines by advancing his own Pawns and forcing Pawn exchanges. Thus, after Blacks plays . . . P—KN3, White may reply P—KR4 and P—KR5, exchanging Pawns and thus opening the King Rook file for attack. Or, after White plays P—KR3, Black may react with . . . P—KN4 and . . . P—KN5, likewise obtaining an open file for attack.

Once the attacker succeeds in forcing open a line leading to the castled position, he has enormously improved his prospects of taking the hostile King by storm. As long as the Pawns remain on their original squares, they form a road block for the attacking pieces. After one of the Pawns has advanced, the barrier is much more likely to be breached —by exchanges, by sacrifices, by violent line-opening.

To sum up: you have seen that Pawn advances in front of the castled King can be weakening—even dangerous. You should therefore avoid such advances. Sometimes you are forced to make such advances—but at least you can avoid making them needlessly. *Avoid such Pawn moves if it is at all possible to avoid them!*

Queen-side castling, which we rarely encounter, presents difficulties for the inexperienced player. The castled King has a wider area to guard than on the King-side. Hence the temptation to meet threats with Pawn advances is much stronger in the case of Queen-side castling. This makes it more likely for the defense on this broader front to be upset by violent sacrifices.

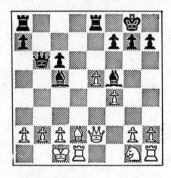

5

BLACK TO MOVE

White's Queen-side castled position is shaky, menaced as it is by Black's Bishops and the open Queen Knight file. Right now the castled Pawn position is intact, but Black's masterly probing soon creates weaknesses that pave the way for brilliant sacrifices.

1	B—Q5!	2 P—B3	QR—N1!

3 P—QN3   KR—Q1!

For *if 4 PxB, then 4 . . . QxQP wins at once.* White's weakened castled position is now riddled with weaknesses.

4 N—B3   QxP!!!

Beautiful play, made possible by the Pawn weaknesses.

5 PxQ   RxP

Threatens mate.

6 B—K1   B—K6ch!!   Resigns

Black mates next move. A convincing demonstration of the disastrous effect of weakening Pawn moves.

6

WHITE TO MOVE
*Black's castled position has been
sadly weakened. His King Rook Pawn
is gone; his King Knight Pawn has
had to advance. Meanwhile White has
established a menacing Pawn wedge
at KB6, and all his pieces are admirably poised for an assault on
Black's King. In fact, White forces
mate in three moves!*

1 QxPch!!   ....

A rude shock for Black. But what interests us is this
thought: if White can afford to sacrifice his most valuable
piece, then Black has indeed damaged his King-side fatally
by weakening Pawn moves.

1 ....   PxQ   2 P—B7ch!   ....

The real point of the sacrifice. The long diagonal becomes
completely clear, allowing White to set up a familiar mating
pattern. The Rook on KR3, supported by the Bishop, forms
this mating pattern.

2 ....   QxP   3 R—R8 mate

One of those combinations that are so distinguished in
their artistry that we can play them over again and again
and still enjoy them. And again, observe that what makes
the artistry possible is *the weakening of Black's castled
position.*

Why do players weaken the castled position? Some do
not realize the weakening effect of the moves; others cannot
help themselves. In this case, it was White's earlier threats
that cleverly forced Black to weaken his castled position.

Getting Pinned

THE BEST ADVICE about getting pinned is: Don't!

Pins occur more frequently on the chessboard than any other type of attack. Yet, strangely enough, pins are rarely defined or explained. *A pin is an attack on a piece which screens another piece from attack.* A piece that is pinned is tied down.

7

In the above diagram, Black's Queen pins White's Rook. The Queen attacks the Rook, which in turn screens the White King from attack. The Rook is pinned (tied down to its present square) because a move of the Rook would expose the White King to attack by the Black Queen. (As you know, the laws of chess forbid your making any move that exposes your King to attack by a hostile piece.)

To emphasize the helplessness of White's pinned Rook, let us suppose that it is Black's move, and that he plays . . . N—B7ch forking White's King and Queen. One's first thought is to reply RxN, in order to save the menaced Queen. But the pinned Rook is helpless; *it cannot move.* White, in check, must move his King, losing his Queen by . . . NxR.

The pathetic helplessness of White's Rook in the previous diagram is typical of pins where the screened piece is the King.

Where the screened piece is any other piece but the King, the player subject to the pin has greater freedom of action. If the screened piece is a Queen, Rook, Bishop, or Knight, the pinned piece can *legally* move. But though such a move is legal, it is not necessarily advisable. The move of a pinned piece will generally involve a serious loss of material. This is brought out in the following position:

8

White's Queen, supported by a White Rook, pins Black's Bishop, which is protected only once and cannot be protected additionally. If the Bishop remains on K3, it is lost; if the Bishop moves, the Knight at K2 which it screens is lost. Black can try 1 . . . N—K5, blocking the pin. But after 2 NxN, PxN; 3 QxP the pin is renewed and White also threatens 4 Q—R7 mate.

The most bearable pins, as far as the defender is concerned, are those where the pinned piece is guarded by a Pawn. In such cases, protection is automatic—and cheap. Where the pinned piece has to be guarded by another piece, you can expect trouble. The pinned piece is tied down; the protecting piece is tied down to the defense of the pinned piece. Thus two units are deprived of much of their mobility and therefore of much of their power.

Another point to remember about the pin is its psychological value. The restraining effect of the pin has a depressing effect on the defender. Pinning and restraining are attacking functions and assure a player the initiative. He has a positive goal—to weaken the pinned piece, to pile up pressure on it, to take advantage of its immobility. The player whose piece is pinned is at a disadvantage. He is at his opponent's mercy, and must often look on helplessly while his pinned piece is being undermined.

It follows, therefore, that you should avoid the pinning of your pieces. Once you are pinned, your freedom of action is restricted, and you are exposed to threats that may cost you the game. Just as it is important not to neglect your development in the opening stage, it is equally vital not to allow your pieces to be pinned later on.

9

WHITE TO MOVE
Black's position seems quite secure— until you observe that he· has badly weakened his King-side with . . . P— KN3. White's problem is—how is he to take advantage of this weakness? He solves the problem by means of a brilliant combination.

1 RxB!! QxR

Now Black's Knight is pinned—in a particularly dangerous
way, too. For this Knight is not protected by a Pawn—thanks
to the earlier . . . *P—KN3*. Therefore the pinned Knight
must be guarded by pieces—always a dangerous and costly
procedure.

2 Q—B3 K—N2
3 N/B3—K4!! ....

Beautiful play. By sacrificing another piece White crushes
Black's resistance to the pin.

3 .... PxN 4 NxP Q—K3

If 4 . . . QxN; 5 QxNch, K—N1; 6 B—R6 forcing
checkmate. Again the weakening of Black's King-side tells
against him.

5 BxNch K—N1 6 Q—B4 Resigns

There is no defense to the threatened *Q—R6*. White's pin
was the weapon that smashed Black's King-side.

Failing to Guard
Against Captures

FEW MISTAKES can be more costly in chess than failing to guard against captures. A capture is often the turning point of a game; it may involve gaining a decisive advantage in material or, in some cases, a vastly superior position.

Sometimes a capture is bound up with a sacrificial combination, in which a piece of great value is given up for one of slight value. Such captures are naturally difficult to foresee. Much more common are those situations in which a capture is quite obvious.

Why are such captures overlooked? Probably because they turn up in positions that seem simple and routine; the player's alertness is lulled; he forgets that almost every position in chess has some element of attack and threat. Positions that are simple on the surface will often turn out, on careful scrutiny, to contain a fantastic wealth of intricate details. If you can acquire the faith that almost every chess position, no matter how simple, has its share of tactical possibilities, you are well on the way to overcoming any tendency to overlook captures.

In the game on page 26, Black overlooks a deadly capture that checkmates him on the 13th move. "Who would have dreamt that it was possible!" is the wondering comment of most chessplayers. Well, the player who saw and executed this combination certainly dreamt it was possible. Whether he found the combination by logical reasoning or by a flash of "inspiration," his example is one that we should all imitate.

10

WHITE TO MOVE
Without bothering to look very deeply into the position, White snaps at a loose Pawn. It is curious that he fails to see the crushing though obvious reply. This kind of slip often occurs in positions that look too "simple" to require careful appraisal and calculation.

1 QxRP??   . . . .

This blunder converts a probably drawn position into immediate loss for White.

The chances are that White expected *1 . . . N—K6?* in reply.

In that event, *2 RxR???* allows *2 . . . Q—N7 mate*, while *2 BxN* is answered by *2 . . . RxRch* winning the Exchange. However, White has *2 Q—R5ch!, K—K2; 3 BxN* winning a piece.

But in reply to 1 QxRP?? Black has a devastating alternative:

1 . . . .   NxP!!

If now 2 RxR???, Q—N7 mate.
Or 2 PxN, RxRch and White loses his Bishop as well.

After 1 . . . NxP!!, White resigned. The real finesse of this move lies in the fact that it renders Q—R5ch impossible for White, leaving him without a defense.

QUEEN'S PAWN OPENING

WHITE	BLACK		WHITE	BLACK
1 P—Q4	P—Q4		3 P—KB3	PxP
2 P—K4!?	PxP		4 NxP	. . . .

White has offered a Pawn in the hope of getting a big lead in development. With careful play, Black has nothing to fear.

4	B—N5		5 B—K3	N—QB3
	6 P—B3	P—K4		

After this optimistic reply Black's pieces are driven back. He gets an easier game with *6 . . . P—K3.*

7 P—Q5	N/B3—K2		9 Q—K4	P—KB3
8 Q—R4ch	B—Q2		10 B—Q3	N—N3??

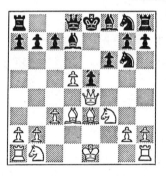

11

Black's last move is quite plausible, and yet it allows a forced mate!

11 QxNch!!!	PxQ		12 BxPch	K—K2
	13 B—B5 mate!			

How did this catastrophe come about? Naturally, Black did not dream that the Queen sacrifice was possible. What features of the position might have helped him to see danger ahead?

In the first place, Black's King is in the center, where, as we know, he is vulnerable. Secondly, the development of his pieces has become tangled up, so that the King can expect no help from his own forces. Finally, Black has advanced the King Bishop Pawn, which opens up a line of approach for White's pieces.

All these factors create danger for Black—but they need not necessarily be fatal. If Black is aware of the difficulty, he will be careful in selecting a Knight move. For example, 10 . . . N—B4 is quite safe and provides relief for the cramped state of Black's pieces. It is the careless 10 . . . N—N3??, played without understanding of the position, that leads to a catastrophe.

Underestimating Your
Opponent's Threats

THREATS are harder to see than captures. Some moves threaten checkmate, some threaten captures, some involve a general improvement in position. Some threats are crude, brutal, obvious. Others are unbelievably subtle in their intentions, refined in their execution. Some threats are sound and directed toward winning the game. Others are based on a foolish idea and will prove disastrous for the player who has devised them. Some threats are irresistible, others can be topped by a stronger threat.

In a game between good players, threats and counterthreats are essentially a matter of interplay of ideas and intentions. If each player does not always see through his opponent's threats, he is at least prepared for them. Thus, as in the case of captures, it is important to realize that threats are always possible, *that they must be looked for.*

That is why threats are most dangerous when they are devised by an opponent who seems to have a lost game. When victory seems within your grasp is just the time when you are most likely to underestimate the other player's resources. "Simple" positions, too, are the downfall of many a player who feels that the game no longer requires careful scrutiny.

Overconfidence is unquestionably the quality that leads many players to overlook their opponents' threats.

12

BLACK TO MOVE

All that Black sees in this position is that one of his Bishops is attacked, and that he can capture the advanced White Knight if he wishes. Yet White threatens one of the most startling brilliancies ever played on the chessboard. Can you see White's threat and how to meet it?

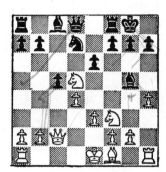

Black's safest course is 1 . . . B—K2 avoiding the opening of the King Rook file and also guarding his Queen Bishop Pawn.

But Black is blind to the explosive possibilities in the position and plays:

| 1 .... | Q—R4ch?? | 2 P—QN4!! | .... |

After this Black can avoid mate only by losing his Queen!

| 2 .... | PxNP | 3 QxPch!!! | .... |

This was White's hidden threat.

| 3 .... | KxQ | 4 PxB dis ch | K—N3 |
| | 5 N—K7 mate | | |

PETROFF'S DEFENSE

WHITE	BLACK		WHITE	BLACK
1 P—K4	P—K4		5 Q—K2	Q—K2
2 N—KB3	N—KB3		6 P—Q3	N—KB3
3 NxP	P—Q3		7 B—N5	B—K3
4 N—KB3	NxP		8 N—B3	QN—Q2

Since neither player can develop his King Bishop, both are likely to castle Queen-side.

9 P—Q4	P—Q4		10 Castles	P—B3

Not good. Since he will probably castle on the Queen-side, the Pawn weakness will endanger Black's castled position.

11 K—N1	P—KR3		12 B—B4!	Castles

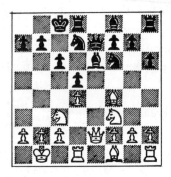

13 Q—R6!!   ....

This unwelcome intrusion was made possible by Black's weakening 10th move. *If now 13 . . . PxQ??; 14 BxQRP mate!*

The fact that Black does not capture the Queen indicates that he sees through this variation. This in turn should give him the key to White's threat—but it doesn't!

13 ....   N—R4??

Best was *13 . . . Q—N5*, countering the threat by preventing the sacrifice which follows:

14 QxBPch!!!   PxQ   15 B—R6 mate!

Another example of the weakening effect of a Pawn advance on the castled position.

Losing A Won Game

Of all the different kinds of mistakes in chess, losing a won game is undoubtedly the most exasperating. No other mistake is more likely to rob you of self-confidence.

What do we mean by a "won game"? When you have a demonstrable mate, a sizable material advantage, a decisive attack, you have a won game. Some advantages are clearer than others; for example, a forced "mate in three" brooks no argument, whereas the advantage of a piece ahead may allow the losing side to play on for a long time.

The ways in which players lose won games can be grouped under a fairly small number of types. Some, when they have an advantage in material, seek complications instead of exchanging remorselessly. As the game simplifies, the excess of material becomes more telling; contrariwise, obscure complications give the prospective loser a chance to turn the tables and befuddle his opponent.

Faulty execution of a winning combination has lost many a game on the very brink of victory. In such cases a player sees the winning idea, plays the winning sacrifice and then inverts the order of his follow-up moves or misses the really clinching point of his combination.

A fault shared by many players is the habit of drifting aimlessly once they have achieved a winning position. Like the man who can't bring himself to say goodbye, they dawdle and delay, seemingly unable to bring the game to a successful conclusion. Even great masters have suffered from this affliction.

Closely related to this psychological handicap is the notion that once a player has achieved a decisive advantage—winning a Rook, for example—he can relax, take it easy, and let nature take its course. This often turns out disastrously, especially against an opponent who is determined and resourceful.

Quite different, but equally unsuccessful, is the player who gives way to despair all too soon. He may even go so far as to resign in a position where he has a quick forced mate!

Most of the faults that turn a won game into a lost one are really aspects of character and temperament. Postmortem analysis shows us what went wrong in the last game, but does not tell us what to do in the next game. To acquire the ability to win won games consistently, you must train yourself to play with determination, to play at all times the best chess of which you are capable, and to give equal care to every type of position.

It will help you to remember that every player has the shattering experience of losing a won game. Every great player owes a good deal of his success to his ability to apply himself to all types of positions; and even the best players have their lapses from time to time.

14

Though White threatens Q—N7 mate, he cannot carry out his threat because of the pin on the King file which wins his Queen. In the actual game, White was so depressed that he resigned. Had he been alert, he would have found a way to force victory in this desperate-looking situation. How?

1 BxPch!   ....

This looks like a "spite check"—the last gasp before resigning.

1 ....   KxB

Forced—not that Black seems to have anything to worry about, as he still maintains the pin.

2 R—KB1ch   K—N1

Again forced. But now White has run out of checks—or so it would seem.

3 R—B8ch!!   ....

Another spite check? No, much better than that—White forces Black to give up the pin on the Queen. Result: White's mating threat comes to life.

3 ....   RxR   4 Q—N7 mate!

Remember, none of this happened! White resigned in the diagramed position, unaware that he had a checkmate within his grasp!

3. HOW TO PLAY THE WHITE PIECES

How to Exploit Your Superior Development

ONE OF our most important tasks in the opening stage is bringing out our pieces so they will play an active and aggressive role.

Because White enjoys the theoretical advantage of moving first, there is always a likelihood that his development will proceed more rapidly than Black's. For White, neglected development may mean nothing worse than *losing the initiative*. For Black, the same sin may mean *losing the game*.

How do players go wrong in the opening? There are certain failings that we observe in game after game. One player moves the same piece again and again, neglecting to develop his other forces and neglecting to get his King into a safe haven.

Another player injudiciously spends time capturing a relatively unimportant Pawn, losing priceless time in the chase.

Other players develop hesitantly and with lack of foresight, moving pieces to squares from which they will be driven away. Soon, to their great astonishment, they find themselves in a straitjacket position which developed inexorably from their poor opening play.

In the first illustrative game White proves that Black's faulty development is definitely a case of too little and too late:

FOUR KNIGHTS' GAME

WHITE	BLACK
1 P—K4	P—K4
2 N—KB3	N—QB3
3 N—B3	N—B3

WHITE	BLACK
4 B—N5	N—Q5
5 NxP	Q—K2
6 N—B3	. . . .

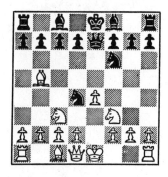

15

White has given his opponent the choice between 6 . . . NxP and 6 . . . NxB. Which is right and which is wrong?

At first glance we feel rather suspicious about Black's procedure. He has moved his Queen Knight twice, and he has played out his Queen very early.

These moves are not quite so bad as they seem. The repeated moves of White's King Knight have canceled out the Black Knight's loss of time.

The position of the Black Queen is definitely bad. Black should therefore play 6 . . . NxB; 7 NxN, QxPch. This forces the exchange of Queens, so that Black no longer suffers from the disadvantage of having developed his Queen too early.

6	NxKP?
7 Castles!	NxQN
8 QPxN	NxNch

9 QxN	Q—B4
10 R—K1ch	B—K2
11 B—Q3	. . . .

White has powerful pressure. He is ahead in development, and if Black castles, White replies 12 Q—K4! winning a piece because Black has no time to guard his menaced Bishop on account of the mating threat.

11	P—Q4		13 B—KB4	Q—KB3
12 B—K3	Q—Q3		14 QxP!!	....

16

Can White afford to offer the Bishop?

The capture 14 . . . QxB? would lead to disaster because of 15 B—N5ch! Thus if 15 . . . K—B1; 16 Q—Q8ch!! and mate next move.

Or 14 . . . QxB?; 15 B—N5ch!, P—QB3; 16 BxPch, PxB; 17 QxQBPch winning the Queen Rook with easy victory in sight.

White has a powerful attack because Black's botched development has exposed the Black King to frightful dangers.

14	P—B3		15 Q—K4	B—K3
16 QR—Q1!	Castles(Q)?			

White has disguised his attacking plan so subtly that Black is lulled into a false sense of security.

(see Diagram 17 on page 38)

17 QxBPch!!	PxQ	18 B—QR6 mate	

17

White has set an incredibly sly trap!

In this game White brought about Black's downfall by exploiting his thoughtless development or no development. In the following game, Black goes Pawn-hunting, while White goes King-hunting. In this unequal struggle White naturally holds all the trumps.

EVANS GAMBIT DECLINED

WHITE	BLACK		WHITE	BLACK
1 P—K4	P—K4		4 P—QN4!?	B—N3
2 N—KB3	N—QB3		5 P—QR4	. . . .
3 B—B4	B—B4			

18

White threatens to win a piece with P—R5 etc.

The opening moves are extremely interesting. On move 4

White offered a Pawn in order to divert Black's pieces and gain time. (The further course of the game will show what White had in mind.)

But Black was not obliging. He simply retreated his attacked Bishop, wisely avoiding complications that might prove exceedingly troublesome.

However, in playing 5 P—QR4 White poses a new problem. If Black keeps his wits about him, he can react calmly with 5 . . . P—QR3! so that if 6 P—R5, B—R2. In that case his Bishop is perfectly safe and White has made no headway.

Instead, Black becomes rattled and goes in for an orgy of Pawn captures. This is just what White was waiting for.

5	....	NxP?		9 Castles	PxP
6	P—R5	B—B4		10 Q—N3	Q—K2
7	P—B3	N—QB3		11 NxP	P—Q3
8	P—Q4	PxP		12 B—KN5	Q—Q2

White is considerably ahead in development as a result of Black's time-wasting Pawn captures. Black's position is already seriously compromised.

Thus, if he tries 12 . . . P—B3 White wins by 13 BxN, PxB; 14 N—Q5, Q—Q1; 15 N—N6!!

Another unpleasant possibility is 12 . . . N—B3; 13 N—Q5, Q—Q1; 14 NxNch, PxN; 15 BxPch etc.

13 P—K5!	PxP		15 NxN	BxN
14 QR—Q1!	N—Q5		16 KR—K1	Q—B4

With all his pieces in action against only two Black pieces, White must win. White's King is quite safe, Black's King is in mortal danger.

19

White's Rooks are all-powerful on the center files.

17 BxPch!	QxB	18 RxPch!	Resigns

For if 18 . . . BxR; 19 R—Q8 mate.

And if 18 . . . K—B1; 19 Q—N4ch, P—B4; 20 RxB!, PxQ; 21 R—Q8ch, Q—K1; 22 R/K5xQch, K—B2; 23 N—K4. White comes out at least a piece ahead.

White's vigorous reaction to Black's ill-judged Pawn-grabbing was very instructive.

In the next game White demonstrates that thoughtless moves ruin Black's prospects of achieving a satisfactory development.

KING'S INDIAN DEFENSE

WHITE	BLACK	WHITE	BLACK
1 P—Q4	N—KB3	8 P—KR3	B—K3?
2 P—QB4	P—KN3	9 P—Q5	PxP
3 N—QB3	B—N2	10 BPxP	B—Q2
4 P—K4	P—Q3	11 Castles	N—K1
5 P—KN3	Castles	12 B—K3	P—N3?
6 B—N2	P—B3	13 P—B4	P—B3?
7 KN—K2	P—K4		

What are the factors that have provided White with such a splendid position?

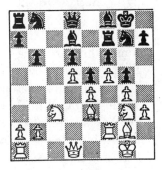

20

White has brilliant encirclement plans —Black's pieces face a dreary prospect.

Black has played thoughtlessly. His eighth move was a futile provocation which lost time. The retreat 11 . . . N—K1 makes sense if followed up by . . . P—B4 fighting for a foothold in the center.

But Black completely overlooks the possibility of playing . . . P—B4. First he wastes more time with 12 . . . P—N3? and then he plays the timid, self-blocking 13 . . . P—B3? His pieces have no future and no scope.

White's indicated strategy is to tie up Black's position still more, and that is exactly what he does.

| 14 P—B5! | P—KN4 | 16 N—N3 | B—KB1 |
| 15 P—KN4 | R—B2 | 17 R—B2 | N—N2 |

21

White can go ahead with his plan, for though Black has rearranged his pieces, they have become even more ineffectual than before.

When you have an advantage in space and mobility—as

White has here—the indicated course is to increase that advantage. White therefore plays to open up the King Rook file, *which will become his exclusive property.*

18	B—KB1!	B—K1
19	R—R2	P—QR4
20	P—KR4!	P—R3

21	PxP	RPxP
22	Q—B3!	R—N2
23	Q—R1!	. . . .

Now that White monopolizes the open King Rook file, he is able to penetrate into Black's position with fatal effect.

22

White's attack must succeed: Black's pieces are posted too awkwardly to have any defensive value.

23	. . . .	N—Q2
24	R—R8ch	K—B2

25	Q—R7	K—K2
26	N—R5	Resigns

For if 26 . . . BxN; 27 PxB and there is no defense against White's coming P—R6 which will win a piece. White's logical and consistent play in this game is a perfect example of how to demolish a cramped position.

In this game White's prime task was to refute a development that was planless. White's hard-hitting play left Black with a middle game position which offered no hope of unscrambling his pieces.

In the next game Black embarks on a devilishly plausible counterattack. But White has a surprising refutation.

QUEEN'S GAMBIT DECLINED

WHITE	BLACK		WHITE	BLACK
1 P—Q4	P—Q4		5 N—B3	PxP
2 P—QB4	P—K3		6 P—K4	P—B4
3 N—KB3	N—KB3		7 BxP	PxP
4 B—N5	B—N5ch		8 NxP	Q—R4

23

Does White have a lost game as a result of Black's powerful-looking Queen move?

Black threatens to win a piece by . . . QxB or by . . . BxNch. But White has an extremely subtle defense!

9 BxN!	BxNch		11 K—B1	QxBch
10 PxB	QxBPch		12 K—N1	. . . .

Now we can appreciate the depth of White's plan:

Black is just on the point of playing 12 . . . PxB with a piece to the good. But he realizes that White would continue 13 R—B1 attacking the Queen with decisive effect.

So Black concludes that he must refrain from "winning a piece" as he finally perceives the far-reaching effect of White's resourceful ninth move.

Black thought he was seizing the initiative. Actually it is White who is doing the attacking, and he presses his advantage vigorously.

12	N—Q2		14 BxP	KR—N1
13 R—B1!	Q—R3		15 B—R6	. . . .

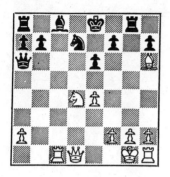

24

White has shattered Black's position.

Thanks to White's ingenious play, the result of Black's Queen moves is that his Queen is shunted off to the side. White has seen to it that Black's King cannot possibly find a safe haven, and that his pieces cannot co-operate effectively.

White's King is quite safe and his King Rook will soon be developed in unorthodox fashion. Meanwhile White has his eye on the most serious weakness in Black's game: his isolated and indefensible King Rook Pawn.

15	N—B3	18 Q—B2!	R—N3
16 P—K5	N—Q4	19 P—R5!	R—N5
17 P—KR4!	B—Q2		

White has left Black no choice, for if 19 . . . RxB; 20 Q—Q2! wins the Rook!

Thus White succeeds in capturing the weak King Rook Pawn, which in turn gives him a menacing passed Pawn. *Black cannot put up proper resistance because his faulty development has split his forces.*

| 20 QxP | K—K2 | 22 B—N7! | Q—R6 |
| 21 R—R4! | KR—N1 | 23 B—B6ch! | K—B1 |

White's coming attack, which relies on the power of the

mighty passed Pawn, cannot be stemmed by Black's disorganized forces.

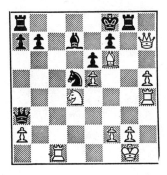

25

White can now play 24 R—B7!! for if 24 . . . NxR; 25 P—R6!! and Black is helpless against 26 QxRch!! and 27 P—R7ch etc.

24 R—B7!!	NxB	25 PxN	Q—Q3
	26 P—R6!!	Resigns	

There is no defense to the coming 27 Q—N7ch!!

With this sparkling example we conclude the study of faulty development and how it can be exploited. The faulty development has taken different forms, but in each case White's resulting initiative has led to a quick decision. Study the procedure in each of these games and you will find opportunities to use similar methods in your own games.

How to Exploit Your Superior Mobility

YOU WILL FIND, almost without exception, that when you have the better development, your pieces have more mobility than your opponent's forces. Remember, if you are playing White, that the first move gives you a springboard for getting ahead in development—and for having more mobility than Black has.

Mobility, you must remember, is connected with having a powerful position in the center. The stronger your position in the center, the more mobility your pieces will have. In the following game White emphasizes this point very strongly.

ALEKHINE'S DEFENSE

WHITE	BLACK		WHITE	BLACK
1 P—K4	N—KB3		3 P—Q4	P—Q3
2 P—K5	N—Q4		4 P—QB4	N—N3

Black has developed one piece, White hasn't developed any at all. Yet White has considerable mobility, as his center Pawns dominate the center and many avenues of development are open to his pieces

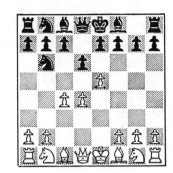

26

Though Black is ahead in development, White has more mobility!

White's immediate aim is to support his powerful Pawn center by advancing his King Bishop Pawn.

5 P—B4	PxP	7 B—K3	B—N2
6 BPxP	P—KN3	8 N—QB3	P—QB4

The advance of Black's Queen Bishop Pawn is logical, as it breaks up the center. (On 9 P—Q5, BxP; 10 BxP Black has a playable though clearly inferior game, as his Knight at Queen Knight 3 is sadly lacking in mobility.)

Instead, Black tries to win a Pawn outright. The attempt is disastrous, because White leaves Black with an unbearably cramped position. White now makes admirably effective use of his superior mobility.

9 P—Q5	Q—B2?	12 NxQPch	K—B1
10 P—Q6!	PxP	13 NxB!	NxN
11 N—N5!	Q—K2	14 BxP!!	Resigns

An extraordinary finish. If 14 . . . QxB; 15 Q—Q8 mate. Thus White wins the Queen by force.

White succeeded admirably in this game because Black started an attack on White's center and failed to follow it up. This gave White time to exploit his superior mobility to the utmost.

27

White is still behind in development and ahead in mobility.

The remaining games in this chapter are more orthodox, for White has superior development, superior mobility, and control of the center in each case.

FRENCH DEFENSE

WHITE	BLACK		WHITE	BLACK
1 P—K4	P—K3		3 N—QB3	PxP
2 P—Q4	P—Q4		4 NxP	. . . .

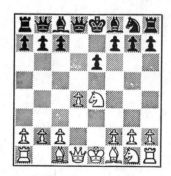

28

White's dominating position in the center makes it likely that he will have vastly superior mobility in the middle game.

White has a free hand in the center, thanks to Black's colorless third move.

White's Knight is strongly centralized at King 4; his Queen Pawn controls the important center square King 5.

4	N—Q2	7 Castles	NxN
5 N—KB3	KN—B3	8 BxN	N—B3
6 B—Q3	B—K2	9 B—Q3	....

White's game is noticeably freer.

9	P—QN3?	11 N—B6	Q—Q3
10 N—K5!	Castles	12 Q—B3!	....

Very clever. White threatens to win a whole Rook by 13 NxBch.

If 12 . . . B—N2?; 13 NxBch and White wins a piece.

Black must therefore develop his Queen Bishop to Queen 2, where it has no mobility. Thus White's lead in mobility becomes even more pronounced.

12	B—Q2	15 KR—K1	KR—K1
13 NxBch	QxN	16 Q—R3!	....
14 B—KN5	QR—B1		

Now White threatens 17 BxN followed by 18 QxRPch.

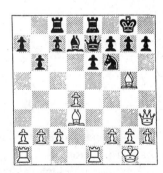

29

White's pressure against Black's King-side is irresistible.

White's superior mobility has provided him with a devastating King-side attack. If now 16 . . . P—KR3; 17 BxP!, PxB; 18 QxRP and Black is helpless against the coming 19 R—K5 and 20 R—KN5ch.

Or if 16 . . . P—N3; 17 Q—R4, K—N2; 18 R—K4! and White's pin leads to Black's downfall after 19 R—KB4.

With his next move Black admits his despair.

16	Q—Q3	19 R—K3	QxP
17 BxN	PxB	20 P—QB3!	Resigns
18 Q—R6!	P—KB4		

If Black retreats 20 . . . Q—N2 or 20 . . . Q—Q3, he must give up his Queen after 21 R—N3. Otherwise, White forces checkmate with 21 R—N3ch etc.

White had an overwhelming advantage in mobility from the third move on as a result of Black's passive play.

In the following game Black fights hard to maintain his grip on the center. But his development is slow and cramped, and White plays with masterly consistency for domination of the open lines.

PHILIDOR'S DEFENSE

WHITE	BLACK	WHITE	BLACK
1 P—K4	P—K4	5 B—QB4	B—K2
2 N—KB3	P—Q3	6 Castles	P—B3
3 P—Q4	N—KB3	7 P—QR4	. . . .
4 N—B3	QN—Q2		

White has already put his finger on the weakness of Black's position:

The development selected by Black is slow, clumsy, and cramped. White notes especially the lack of mobility of Black's Bishops. His King Bishop is blocked by his Queen's Pawn; his Queen Bishop is blocked by his Queen Knight.

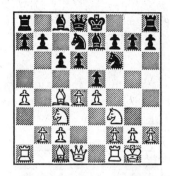

30

White has an advantage in the fact that Black's Bishops have very little scope.

White's policy from now on will be to create more open lines for his own forces and at the same time to restrain Black from freeing himself.

7	Q—B2	12 N—R4!	N—R4
8 Q—K2	P—KR3	13 N—B5	B—B1
9 B—R2	N—B1	14 B—K3	P—KN3
10 Q—B4!	N—K3	15 QR—Q1!!	....
11 PxP	PxP		

White's last move looks like an oversight, but it isn't. He loses no time occupying the open Queen file, even though his Knight is attacked.

This is how White reasons:

As Black has not yet castled, he is unable to bring a Rook to the Queen file to dispute White's occupation of that open line.

Furthermore, because Black's King is still in the center, he cannot hope to win a piece with impunity. Thus if 15 . . . PxN; 16 PxP, N—Q1; 17 N—Q5!, Q—R4; 18 N—N6!!, PxN; 19 RxNch!, KxR; 20 QxKBP and Black's King perishes in the crossfire of the enemy pieces.

This fascinating variation, which deserves the most careful study, is a magnificent example of White's power of superior mobility.

15	...	B—Q2		18 P—B4!	PxP
16	N—N3	N—B3		19 BxBP	Q—N3ch
17	P—R3	B—N2		20 K—R1	N—R2

White has increased his mobility still more by opening the King Bishop file. Thus he is ready for action on two open files.

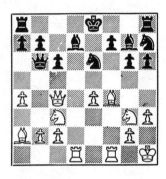

31

White can now win by a very brilliant combination.

21 RxB!   KxR   22 B—K3!! QR—KB1

He might just as well resign. If 22 . . . QxB; 23 RxPch, K—Q1; 24 QxN forces mate.

23 RxPch!!   Resigns

For if 23 . . . RxR; 24 QxNch, K—Q1; 25 BxQch, PxB; 26 QxR and Black is hopelessly behind in material.   -

White's play was a masterpiece of consistently utilizing superior mobility. From the very start White took merciless advantage of Black's lack of mobility. He never gave Black a chance because he never allowed Black's pieces to cooperate properly.

In the next game White neatly combines superior mobility with control of the center and lasting King-side attack.

QUEEN'S GAMBIT

WHITE	BLACK		WHITE	BLACK
1 P—Q4	P—Q4		3 N—KB3	N—KB3
2 P—QB4	PxP		4 N—B3	P—K3

White now seizes on the fact that with his second move
Black has given up his hold on the center. Black should therefore play . . . P—B4 as soon as possible in order to fight for
a foothold in the center. Because he holds back timidly, White
gains an overwhelming position in the center by energetic play.

5 B—N5!	B—K2		8 BxP	N—Q2
6 P—K4!	P—KR3?		9 Castles	Castles
7 BxN	BxB		10 P—K5!	B—K2

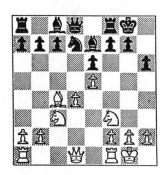

32

*White's formation is aggressive, while
the outlook for Black's pieces is very
poor.*

White has driven a wedge into Black's position by advancing his King Pawn to King 5. One important consequence is
that he has prevented Black from bringing his Knight to King
Bishop 3. This is the best square for a Knight defending the
King-side. It follows that the combination of White's aggressive position in the center, plus the aggressive position of his
pieces, foreshadows a powerful attack by White.

Note in the following play how White uses the square King
4 as a steppingstone for transporting his pieces to the King-

side. We know from the start that his onslaught will be successful because Black has so little maneuvering space for defensive purposes.

11 Q—K2	R—K1	14 KR—K1	N—B1
12 QR—Q1!	P—QB3	15 Q—N4	P—QN3
13 Q—K4!	Q—B2	16 Q—R5	B—N2

The position begins to look very threatening for Black. White now proceeds to bring more pieces to the King-side. Because of the cramped position of his forces, Black cannot defend with equal vigor.

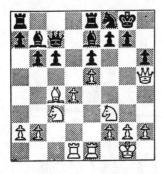

33

White again gets more pieces into the attack by using the square King 4.

17 R—K4!	B—N5	20 N—N5!	R—K2
18 R—N4	BxN	21 N—K4!	R—Q1
19 PxB	K—R1	22 R—Q3!	P—QB4

At last Black plays the move that he should have played early in the opening. But White is now ready for the final attack, having maneuvered his Knight into position for a deadly stroke. He has also moved his Queen Rook into position for the final attack.

23 N—B6!   . . . .

With the brutal threat 24 QxRPch!!, PxQ; 25 R—N8 mate. White's superior mobility has become overwhelming.

Of course, if Black tries 23 . . . PxN then 24 QxRPch and 25 Q—N7 mate.

| 23 .... | N—N3 | 24 R—R3 | Resigns |

34

White has left Black no move to hold the position.

White's overwhelming plus in mobility has left Black without any satisfactory defense.

Thus if 24 . . . PxN; 25 QxPch, K—N1; 26 Q—R8 mate.

Or 24 . . . PxP; 25 Q—N5!!, QxB; 26 RxPch!, PxR; 27 QxP mate.

White never gave Black a chance after Black's all too passive handling of the opening.

In the following game White again triumphs after dominating the center and preventing Black from getting his pieces into action. White's Pawn-storming attack follows with crushing—and logical—effect.

SICILIAN DEFENSE

WHITE	BLACK	WHITE	BLACK
1 P—K4	P—QB4	3 P—Q4	PxP
2 N—KB3	P—Q3	4 NxP	. . . .

White has a well centralized Knight established at Queen 4. Black cannot imitate this maneuver. Note also that White controls the important center square Queen 5 with his King Pawn.

On these two grounds it seems likely that White will dominate the center and will therefore enjoy superior mobility.

35

There are already strong indications that White may achieve an overwhelming plus in mobility.

4	....	N—KB3
5	N—QB3	N—B3
6	B—K2	P—K3

| 7 | B—K3 | B—K2 |
| 8 | Castles | Castles |

How has the situation developed as regards mobility? Both White Bishops have free diagonals; both Black Bishops are hemmed in by Pawns. The outlook for Black's game is very unpromising.

In such positions White always has a practical problem: *how can his superior mobility be increased still further?* White solves this problem by a general advance of his King-side Pawns, which will achieve the following:

1. He will congest Black's position more than ever.

2. He will drive away Black's King Knight—his best defensive piece—from King Bishop 3.

3. He will subject Black's position, already cramped unbearably, to a devastating Pawn-storming attack.

9	P—B4	Q—B2
10	P—KN4!	P—QR3
11	P—N5	N—K1

12	P—B5	Q—Q1
13	P—KR4	NxN
14	QxN	....

White's plan has made considerable progress. As a result of Black's unpromising opening line of play, White has deprived Black of any constructive plan.

36

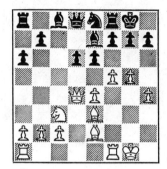

The formidable centralization of White's Queen provokes Black to lose his foothold in the center.

14 ....   P—K4?

Very shortsighted. He drives away the Queen, but at the cost of permanently losing Pawn control of his Queen 4 square.

This vital center square now becomes a "hole," completely at the mercy of the White pieces.

| 15 Q—Q2 | N—B2 | 17 R—B2 | B—Q1 |
| 16 B—N6! | Q—Q2 | 18 QR—KB1 | .... |

White menaces a decisive breach with 19 P—B6, P—N3; 20 P—R5. Black stops this, but White penetrates in a different way.

| 18 .... | P—B3 | 20 P—N6! | P—R3 |
| 19 B—B4ch | K—R1 | 21 B—B7 | Q—B3 |

White can now win by 22 B—K3 and 23 BxP! He plans a much more striking finish.

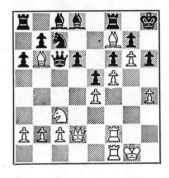

37

There is no defense against White's coming attack.

| 22 BxN | BxB | 23 R—N2! | P—Q4 |

Desperation.

24 QxRPch!!   Resigns

For if 24 . . . PxQ; 25 P—N7ch, K—R2 and now White captures the Rook, promoting to a Knight (!) and giving checkmate after 25 . . . K—R1; 26 R—N8ch!

The games in this chapter teach a lesson of the greatest practical importance—that when White gets the initiative through superior mobility, he has a lasting advantage that he can increase systematically until he achieves victory.

The first step is to pinpoint Black's faulty strategy. Once you see how he has committed himself to a cramped position, you can find ways to increase your command of the board. You must not swerve from your determination to keep him in a vise; one thoughtless move will often allow the enemy to escape. All five games in this chapter show how you maintain and increase the pressure until Black's position collapses.

Opening Mistakes White Should Avoid

So FAR you have seen the methods by which White exploits Black's mistakes in the opening and the early middle game. *These methods are valid and useful as long as White does not violate the rules of good opening play.*

It is therefore vital for you to be forewarned against the danger of losing the initiative when you play White.

This danger comes from neglect of your development. You may damage your development by losing time or by developing pieces inefficiently.

There are some openings in which the defects are so obvious that these openings have been partly or completely discredited. Many years ago, when opening theory was not so well understood as it is today, some of these openings were popular. In the course of time their serious defects became all too clear. Such openings are described in Chapter Eight but here we want to emphasize several of them, pointing out their defects in some detail:

The Center Game offers a good example. Here are the opening moves:

WHITE	BLACK
1 P—K4	P—K4
2 P—Q4	PxP
3 QxP	N—QB3

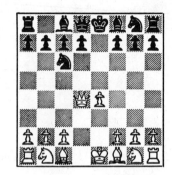

38

White's Queen must retreat with loss of time.

Black's last move gains time by attacking the Queen. White must now move the Queen out of attack, giving Black another tempo for development. What usually happens is that White plays 4 Q—K3 and Black replies 4 . . . N—B3, developing another piece.

To understand what has happened, you must realize that in effect *Black has taken over the role usually held by White.* It is no longer White who is a move ahead; Black has the initiative.

The same mistake on White's part appears in milder form in the Scotch Game:

WHITE	BLACK
1 P—K4	P—K4
2 N—KB3	N—QB3
3 P—Q4	. . . .

To advance in the center and to open up a line for the Queen Bishop seems very good on general principles. But the advance of the Queen Pawn is not well timed.

| 3 . . . . | PxP |
| 4 NxP | . . . . |

By recapturing, White moves his Knight a second time and thus wastes a move.

Black, by way of reply, develops with gain of time. He can

play 4 . . . B—B4, developing a new piece and gaining time by threatening to win White's Knight.

Or Black can play 4 . . . N—B3, likewise developing a new piece and gaining time by threatening to win White's King Pawn.

4 . . . .   N—B3

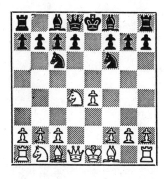

39

White is on the defensive: he must defend his King Pawn.

In this case White's shortcomings are not fatal. However, any possibility of keeping Black's position under pressure is gone.

Another kind of mistake to avoid with the White pieces is to develop inefficiently. Note this in Alapin's Opening:

WHITE	BLACK
1 P—K4	P—K4
2 N—K2	. . . .

As you know, White almost invariably plays 2 N—KB3. You may have wondered why White should not play 2 N—K2. There are two reasons for this.

On King 2 the Knight blocks the development of White's King Bishop and thus holds up White's whole development. Furthermore, N—K2 is passive whereas N—KB3 is aggressive, attacking Black's King Pawn.

In view of these defects, N—K2 is ruled out as a worthwhile move.

40

White's last move was much too passive.

A similar example appears in Ponziani's Opening:

	WHITE	BLACK
1	P—K4	P—K4
2	N—KB3	N—QB3
3	P—B3	. . . .

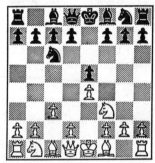

41

White's last move blocks his development.

White's last move deprives his Queen Knight of its best square. Black replies 3 . . . P—Q4! opening up the position favorably. After 4 PxP, QxP White is unable to attack the Black Queen by 5 N—B3, because 3 P—B3 has made the Knight move impossible.

As in the previous examples, Black has an easy time of it. Black has the initiative and has nothing to fear. From the positions discussed in this chapter, you can see that White must avoid *loss of time as well as ineffectual development*. If White violates these simple rules, *he loses his chance to exploit Black's mistakes in the opening*.

4. HOW TO PLAY THE BLACK PIECES

How to Seize the Initiative

IF YOU ACCEPT the view that White has some initiative by reason of being the first to move, you will doubtless agree that in actual practice White often loses that initiative with great rapidity.

When you are playing Black, you can snatch up White's lost initiative and become the aggressor, if you realize just what is happening.

Now, assuming that White does not lose material and does not create weaknesses, just what should Black look for in order to seize the initiative?

There are several ways White can go wrong. He may, for example, play an opening so poor that his theoretical advantage disappears at once. This gives Black his chance.

Or White may play an excellent opening and then ruin his development by a series of foolish, time-wasting Queen moves. Here again Black must be alert to the possibilities.

If Black discovers that White is wasting valuable time chasing a relatively unimportant Pawn, he can use the opportunity to get far ahead in development.

Sometimes White may avoid the sin of greed only to succumb to another fault—bad judgment. Sheer thoughtlessness, inattention, negligence, or happy-go-lucky innocence of a positional trap may ruin White's development. In every case Black should be alert to seize the initiative.

So you see there are many ways for White to go wrong,

and it pays Black to keep a sharp lookout for such cases of poor judgment. Now let's see some examples of the kinds of mistakes White may make.

In this game Black gives us a classic example of slashing attacking play. His play is magnificent, and yet—it all stems from White's faulty opening. Black immediately pounces on the opportunities offered by White's faulty play.

Lost Initiative from a Poor Opening

IRREGULAR OPENING

WHITE	BLACK		WHITE	BLACK
1 P—QN4	P—K3		2 B—N2	N—KB3

Even at this early stage we can see the faulty character of White's first move. Black is attacking, White is defending! Black's development will proceed rapidly, while White's will be laborious.

3 P—QR3	P—B4		4 P—N5	P—Q4

Black's Pawns already have a substantial foothold on the center, while White has no Pawns in the center at all. His attempt to improve the situation leads to disaster.

5 P—Q4?   . . . .

Plausible but weak, as Black promptly proves.

42

Black now seizes the initiative.

5 ....   Q—R4ch!

This forceful move starts a chain reaction. It forces White
to play N—QB3 in order to protect his unfortunate Queen
Knight Pawn. Then, to protect this Knight, White is forced
to develop his Queen in a risky manner. These factors give
Black his chance for a brilliant attack.

| 6 N—QB3 | N—K5 | 8 QxP | B—B4! |
| 7 Q—Q3 | PxP | 9 QxNP | BxPch |

Black's brisk attacking play has shunted White's Queen
far from the scene of action and has deprived White's King
of the castling privilege. Even at this early stage White's
position is shattered.

10 K—Q1   ....

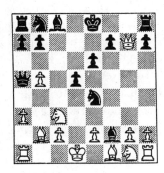

43

*How does Black guard his menaced
Rook?*

10 ....   P—Q5!!

Black ignores the attack on his Rook because he has decided on an all-out attack on the White King. Note, by the
way, that 11 NxN? allows 11 ... Q—K8 mate!

| 11 QxRch | K—K2! | 12 QxB | PxN |

In the event of 13 BxP Black intends 13 . . . NxBch; 14
K—Q2, N—K5 dbl ch; 15 K—Q3, Q—Q7ch; 16 KxN,
Q—K6 mate.

13 B—B1   N—Q2!!

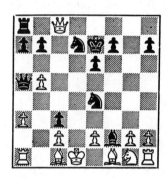

44

Black offers another Rook!

Thus, if White now plays 14 Q—B4, Black would reply
with . . . R—Q1, and the game would develop as follows:
15 Q—N4ch, QN—B4 dis ch!; 16 B—Q2, RxBch; 17 K—
B1, R—Q8ch!!; 18 KxR, Q—Q1ch followed by mate.

What now follows is a foregone conclusion, despite White's
enormous material advantage. With four powerful attacking
pieces at his disposal, Black engineers a sparkling mating
attack.

14 QxR	QxNP	16 K—B1	B—K6ch!!
15 B—B4	Q—Q4ch	17 BxB	N—B7!!

White resigns, for after 18 BxN Black replies 18 . . .
Q—Q7ch forcing mate in two more moves.

Black has forcefully punished White for losing the initiative by choosing an inferior opening line.

In the next game White starts out with an excellent opening; but then, animated by some perverse suicidal impulse, he lets his Queen drift out of play. Black develops rapidly and forcefully, sacrifices both Rooks, and wins handsomely.

Lost Initiative from too Many Queen Moves

NIMZOINDIAN DEFENSE

WHITE	BLACK		WHITE	BLACK
1 P—Q4	N—KB3		5 PxP	N—R3
2 P—QB4	P—K3		6 P—QR3	BxNch
3 N—QB3	B—N5		7 QxB	NxP
4 Q—B2	P—B4		8 B—N5	P—QR4

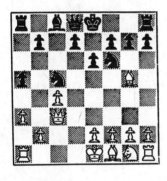

45

A typical situation in the Nimzoindian Defense.

This position is typical of the opening because Black has developed rapidly but has had to give up one of his Bishops in the process.

White should now play 9 P—B3, P—R5; 10 P—K4, P—Q3 leading to a position with chances for both sides. Instead, his weak play enables Black to seize the initiative.

9 Q—K5?	P—Q3		11 Q—B4?	P—K4
10 BxN	PxB		12 Q—R6	Q—N3!

Black has gained two moves for developing his Bishop and

has also brought his Queen into active play. White belatedly returns to rational moves, but as Black demonstrates, it is already too late for that.

| 13 R—N1 | B—B4!! | | 15 QxRch | K—K2 |
| 14 QxBP | BxR | | 16 QxR | .... |

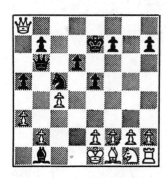

46

Black has a mating attack.

This is the position Black has played for: White's Queen is far afield, and his other pieces are still on their home squares.

$$16 .... \quad N—K5!$$

Threatens mate in two.

$$17 P—K3 \quad QxNP$$

Threatening mate on the move.

$$18 QxRP \quad QxBPch$$

White resigns, for if 19 K—Q1, QxBch; 20 Q—K1, Q—Q6ch and mate next move. Black has played with superb energy to exploit White's nerveless loss of the initiative.

In the next game, also, White plays the opening not too badly but Black maneuvers ingeniously to obtain the advantage when White becomes greedy.

Lost Initiative from Greedy Play

FRENCH DEFENSE

WHITE	BLACK		WHITE	BLACK
1 P—K4	P—K3		5 B—Q3	B—Q3
2 P—Q4	P—Q4		6 Castles	Castles
3 PxP	PxP		7 N—B3	N—B3
4 N—KB3	N—KB3		8 B—KN5	. . . .

White has already forfeited part of his initiative by playing 3 PxP and thereby opening the diagonal of Black's imprisoned Queen Bishop. Nevertheless, Black is still under some pressure, mainly because his King Knight is pinned and his Queen Pawn is under attack.

47

How is Black to defend his Queen Pawn?

Black's daring conclusion is that he need not defend his Queen Pawn altogether! Therefore he plays:

8 ....   B—KN5!

The first point of Black's play is that if 9 NxP, BxPch; 10 KxB, QxN and he has recovered the Pawn with a good game.

  9 BxN   QxB!   10 NxP   Q—R3!

Now Black threatens 11 . . . BxN and 12 . . . QxP mate.

Nor can White defend with 11 P—KN3?, for then 11 . . . Q—R4! wins.

True, White can play 11 Q—B1, but after 11 . . . QxQ; 12 QRxQ, BxN; 13 PxB, NxP Black has regained his Pawn and has a very promising endgame. White therefore selects what *seems* to be the least evil:

11 P—KR3   ....

48

Black has seized the initiative.

11 ....   NxP!

Black offers a piece that cannot be accepted, for if 12 PxB???, NxNch; 13 QxN, Q—R7 mate.

  12 B—K2   NxNch   13 BxN   BxP!

Black, who gave up a Pawn a few moves ago, is now actually a Pawn ahead. White cannot play 14 PxB because of 14 . . . QxP; 15 R—K1, B—R7ch; 16 K—R1, B—N6 dis ch; 17 K—N1, Q—R7ch and mate next move.

14 R—K1	B—K3	16 Q—K2	BxN
15 P—KN3	QR—Q1	17 BxB	BxP!

A neat thrust. If 18 PxB, RxB with a second Pawn to the good.

18 B—K4	R—Q7	19 QxR	B—R7ch!

White resigns, for if 20 K—N2, QxQ; 21 KxB, QxKBPch with a tremendous advantage in material for Black.

It was fascinating to see how cleverly Black snatched the initiative and the attack in this bright little game. In the next game all is tranquil throughout, but the game is if anything even more instructive.

Lost Initiative from Blocked Development

FOUR KNIGHTS' GAME

WHITE	BLACK	WHITE	BLACK
1 P—K4	P—K4	4 B—N5	B—N5
2 N—KB3	N—QB3	5 Castles	Castles
3 N—B3	N—B3	6 BxN	. . . .

If Black plays 6 . . . NPxB?, he will create lasting difficulties for himself, because his Queen Bishop will no longer be able to develop. However, he uses his Queen Pawn to recapture. This enables the Bishop to develop effectively.

49

How should Black retake?

6	QPxB!		8 B—N5	P—KR3
7 P—Q3	B—Q3		9 B—R4	P—B4!

50

Black has set a subtle trap.

Black's last move not only prevents P—Q4; it also sets a trap into which White falls headlong.

10 N—Q5?   P—KN4!   11 NxNch   ....

Likewise after 11 B—N3, NxN; 12 PxN, B—N5 Black has all the play.

11	QxN		14 QxB	QxQ
12 B—N3	B—N5!		15 PxQ	P—KB3
13 P—KR3	BxN		16 K—N2	....

The result of Black's positional trap is that he is in effect a piece to the good. White's Bishop is a dead piece, and can play no effective role in the game.

| 16 .... | P—QR4 | 18 R—R1 | K—K3 |
| 17 P—QR4 | K—B2 | 19 P—R4 | KR—QN1 |

51

Black is a piece ahead!

Black's strategy is delightfully simple. He plays to open a file on the Queen-side, by advancing . . . P—N4 and . . . P—B5. Then his "extra" piece is bound to win for him.

| 20 PxP | RPxP | 22 R—QR2 | P—N4 |
| 21 P—N3 | P—B3 | 23 KR—R1 | P—B5 |

If now 24 NPxP Black wins easily after 24 . . . PxBP; 25 PxP, R—N5 etc.

24 RPxP	PxP/N6	27 P—Q4	R—N4
25 BPxP	RxP	28 R—B4	R—N5
26 R—R4	RxP	29 RxBP	RxP

White resigns, as he is powerless against Black's "extra" piece. There is a great deal to be learned from the way Black seized the initiative by taking advantage of White's careless 10th move.

In the following game Black sees his opportunity to seize the initiative when White condemns his King Bishop to lasting inactivity. Then Black continues to exercise cumulative pressure on White's weakened position.

Lost Initiative by an Error of Judgment

SICILIAN DEFENSE

WHITE	BLACK		WHITE	BLACK
1 P—K4	P—QB4		6 B—K2	P—K4
2 N—KB3	P—Q3		7 N—N3	B—K3
3 P—Q4	PxP		8 Castles	QN—Q2
4 NxP	N—KB3		9 P—B4	Q—B2
5 N—QB3	P—QR3		10 P—B5?	....

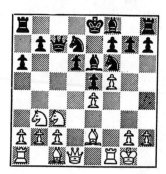

52

Black can now take the initiative.

With Pawns on the white squares King 4 and King Bishop 5, White has reduced the mobility of his King Bishop to an alarming extent. If this piece is not "dead," it is certainly "half-dead." Another drawback to White's last move is that it releases pressure on the center, thereby enabling Black to react eventually with . . . P—Q4!

10	B—B5		13 Q—K2	QR—B1
11 B—Q3	P—QN4!		14 QR—B1	Castles
12 B—K3	B—K2		15 N—Q2	P—Q4!

Declaration of independence. As in the previous game, White's colorless opening has been the first step in Black's seizure of the initiative.

True, Black permits White to get rid of the useless Bishop and cancel Black's pressure on the half-open Queen Bishop file. But Black exacts a heavy price: the opening of the Queen file for Black's forces.

| 16 BxB | QPxB | 18 PxP | BxP |
| 17 P—QR3 | P—N5! | 19 P—N4 | .... |

A gesture toward attack on the King-side. But Black is well prepared for it. The permanent result is a weakness that Black will exploit later on.

19	BxN	23 K—R1	KR—Q1
20 PxB	Q—B3!	24 Q—K2	P—R3
21 Q—N2	N—B4!	25 R—R1	Q—Q3
22 BxN	QxBch	26 KR—Q1	....

53

Black is ready for the final blow.

26 ....   Q—B3!

Black threatens 27 . . . RxN!; 28 RxR, NxKP and wins because of the menace of a murderous discovered check.

If now 27 R—KN1, RxN!; 28 QxR, NxKP; 29 Q—N2, N—B7 mate. Or if 27 R—K1, NxNP! winning a Pawn.

27 K—N2	R—Q3!		29 K—B3	Q—Q2!
28 P—R3	QR—Q1!		30 K—K3	....

54

How does Black add the last bit of pressure that topples White's position?

White has rushed in his King to the center to bolster his position. But Black's mighty pin on the Queen file leaves White helpless while the Black Knight makes a lengthy trip to Queen Knight 4.

30	N—K1!		32 RxKP	N—N4!
31 R—R5	N—B2!		33 R—Q5	....

Losing the Exchange by 33 RxN is even worse.

33	RxR		35 Q—B3	NxRch
34 PxR	NxP		Resigns	

White has no compensation for the loss of the Exchange. Having seized the initiative at an early stage, Black made admirable use of it thereafter.

Thus, in all the games in this chapter, we have seen the various ways that Black can seize the initiative in consequence of faulty play by White.

How to Seize the Attack

SO FAR WE have seen how Black defends, how he reacts to gambits, how he seizes the initiative, how he counter-attacks. Now we want to see situations in which a serious flaw in White's game gives Black a chance for a slashing all-out attack.

One word of warning: when playing the Black pieces, do not embark lightly on an attacking policy. Note in each of the following games that White compromises his game in some fashion, while Black maintains an impeccable position.

Exploiting White's Faulty Development

VIENNA GAME

WHITE	BLACK	WHITE	BLACK
1 P—K4	P—K4	3 P—B4	P—Q4
2 N—QB3	N—KB3	4 BPxP	NxP

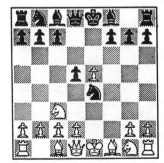

55

Black's Knight is splendidly centralized.

5 N—B3   N—QB3.   6 B—Q3?   P—KB4

White cannot very well play BxN now, as he would lose further time—and his King Pawn as well. He therefore captures Black's King Bishop Pawn in passing. This returns Black's King Knight to the King Bishop 3 square. But meanwhile White's Queen Pawn cannot advance. As a result, White's Queen Bishop and Queen Rook are still on their original squares at the end of the game.

7 PxP e.p.   NxBP   8 Castles   B—B4ch

Development with gain of time. Note that White is unable to reply P—Q4.

9 K—R1   Castles   10 B—N5   N—KN5!

Threatening to win the Exchange by . . . N—B7ch.

If White tries 11 P—Q4, then 11 . . . NxQP; 12 NxN, RxRch; 13 QxR, BxN and Black is a Pawn ahead.

Thus Black wrests another concession from White. In giving up his developed Bishop, White increases Black's lead in development and his attacking prospects.

11 BxN   PxB   12 P—Q4   B—Q3

Black's attack has become very powerful; he threatens to win the Exchange by . . . B—R3.

13 P—KR3   B—R3!!

56

Can Black afford to ignore the attack on his Knight?

14 PxN	BxR	15 QxB	RxN!!

With this sacrifice, Black establishes the soundness of his previous sacrifice. First point: if 16 PxR, Black has a quick mate with 16 . . . Q—R5ch etc.

Second point: if 16 QxR, Q—R5ch—and now if 17 Q—R3, Q—K8 mate. Or 17 K—N1, Q—K8ch; 18 Q—B1, B—R7ch winning White's Queen.

But the best is yet to come.

16 Q—K1 Q—R5ch!!	17 QxQ	R—B8 mate

Thus we see that Black's brilliant attack succeeded because White's Queen Bishop remained at home.

This game is a joy to play over because Black never misses a chance to find an energetic move. His play is forceful but not brash. White, on the other hand, dawdles. First he hits out aimlessly—and then strikes at the wrong target.

Exploiting White's Neglected Development

SCOTCH GAMBIT

WHITE	BLACK	WHITE	BLACK
1 P—K4	P—K4	3 P—Q4	PxP
2 N—KB3	N—QB3	4 B—QB4	N—B3

Ignoring the defense of his Queen Pawn, Black strikes at White's King Pawn.

5 P—K5	. . . .

White, too, intends to attack.

57

How does Black save his Knight?

$$5 \dots \qquad P—Q4!$$

Instead of defending, Black attacks!—and opens up the diagonal of his Queen Bishop at the same time.

6 B—QN5	N—K5	8 NxN	PxN
7 NxP	B—Q2	9 B—Q3	B—QB4

Black's obvious eagerness to attack is perfectly well grounded in the fact that he has two extra pieces in play.

$$10 \ BxN \qquad \dots$$

58

Should Black recapture?

$$10 \dots \qquad Q—R5!$$

The alternative 10 . . . PxB is quite satisfactory, but Black's Queen move brings still another piece into play—threatening mate, by the way.

11 Q—K2   PxB   12 B—K3   B—KN5!

Forcing a crisis, for if 13 Q—Q2 Black leaves his opponent without an adequate reply by playing 13 . . . R—Q1.

13 Q—B4   . . . .

Apparently crushing: if Black moves his attacked Bishop, the Queen fork 14 QxQBPch seems deadly.

13 . . . .   BxB!

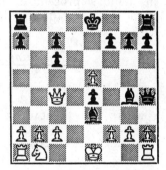

59

Black has started a crisp winning combination.

On 14 QxQBPch Black intends 14 . . . B—Q2!!; 15 QxRch, K—K2!!; 16 QxR and Black forces mate beginning with 16 . . . QxBPch.

Suppose, however, White interpolates 16 P—KN3 in this variation? Then Black wins with 16 . . . BxPch!; 17 KxB, P—K6ch! If now 18 KxP, Q—N4ch wins White's Queen, and if 18 K—N1, P—K7! decides.

Finally, if 18 K—K1, Q—QN5ch; 19 P—B3, QxNP; 20 QxR, B—N5! and Black forces mate.

| 14 P—KN3 | Q—Q1!! | | 16 K—B2 | Q—B6ch |
| 15 PxB | Q—Q8ch | | 17 K—N1 | . . . . |

On 17 K—K1 Black had 17 . . . QxKPch; 18 K—B1, B—R6 mate.

| 17 . . . . | B—R6! | | 19 QxRch | K—K2 |
| 18 QxQBPch | K—B1 | | Resigns | |

White's Queen is *en prise* and he cannot stop mate. Beautiful play by Black.

Sometimes White gets a good development and then embarks on a faulty plan. It takes a sharp eye to see the flaw in White's procedure. In the following delightful game Black takes admirable advantage of White's shortcomings.

Exploiting White's Faulty Plan

GIUOCO PIANO

WHITE	BLACK		WHITE	BLACK
1 P—K4	P—K4		3 B—B4	B—B4
2 N—KB3	N—QB3		4 P—B3	. . . .

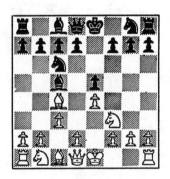

60

Black must decide on his policy in the center.

White intends to play P—Q4. Then, if Black exchanges Pawns, White gets a powerful Pawn center and an ideal development. Black therefore determines to avoid the exchange of Pawns.

4	P—Q3	9 R—K1	Castles
5 Castles	B—N3!	10 P—QN4	K—R1!
6 P—Q4	Q—K2	11 B—R3	N—KN1!
7 P—QR4	P—QR3	12 P—N5	N—R4!
8 P—R3	N—B3	13 NxP	. . . .

Since . . . PxN??? would lose the Queen, Black seems to have blundered. How does he regain his Pawn?

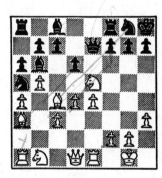

61

Black seizes the attack.

13   . . . .   P—KB3!

With this powerful reply Black completely turns the tables. If the attacked Knight moves, Black wins a piece. Thus he forces White's reply.

14 BxN	BPxN!	15 B—R2	KPxP

If now 16 BPxP, Q—B3 is much in Black's favor.

16 N—Q2   BxP!

How to Seize the Attack · **83**

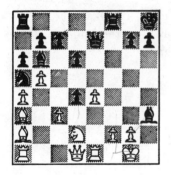

62

Black's surprise sacrifice is only the beginning.

On 17 PxB Black intends 17 . . . Q—N4ch; 18 K—B1, RxPch!!; 19 KxR, P—Q6 dis ch with a crushing attack.

17 N—B3	B—N5	18 BPxP	PxP!

For on 19 PxP Black continues 19 . . . BxN; 20 PxB, Q—N4ch; 21 K—B1, QxPch and is ahead in material.

19 Q—Q3	BxN	21 K—B1	N—B5!
20 PxB	Q—N4ch	22 B—B1	Q—R4
	23 PxP	RxP!!	

63

Black has given his opponent another unpleasant surprise.

The point of Black's last sacrifice is that if 24 QxN, Black wins with 24 . . . R—KR6!

24 BxN	RxR!	25 Q—Q1	RxB!

White resigns, for if QxR/B1, R—KR6! wins.

Opening Mistakes Black Should Avoid

AS WE'VE pointed out earlier, an opening mistake on White's part may cost him the initiative; an opening mistake on Black's part may cost him the game. If Black plays well, White's advantage of the first move will be neutralized from the start; if Black plays badly, White's advantage will result in a quickly winning game.

The Dangers of Thoughtless Development

In the following game Black begins with inexact moves and soon finds himself in a hopeless position:

WHITE	BLACK	WHITE	BLACK
1 P—Q4	P—Q4	2 N—KB3	N—QB3

A doubtful move, because Black needs to advance the Queen Bishop Pawn to free himself.

| | 3 P—B4 | P—K3? |

Again he cramps his game voluntarily. 3 . . . B—N5 is more promising.

| | 4 N—B3 | PxP? |

Now he surrenders the center. Eventually White will react powerfully with P—K4.

5	P—K3	N—B3	9	Q—B2	N—K2
6	BxP	B—N5	10	B—R3	P—B3
7	Castles	BxN?	11	P—K4	P—KR3?
8	PxB	Castles	12	QR—Q1	B—Q2

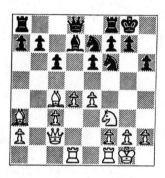

64

Black has played the opening very badly.

Black's thoughtless development has left him in a hopeless position. Blocking his Queen Bishop Pawn on move 2, he is now unable to play the freeing move . . . P—QB4.

Having hemmed in his Queen Bishop on move 3, he has condemned this piece to lasting uselessness.

By surrendering the center on move 4, Black gave his opponent a chance to build up a mighty center.

The exchange on move 7 created a magnificent diagonal for White's Queen Bishop.

On move 11 Black weakened his King-side, making it easier for White to conduct an attack against the Black King.

The Dangers of Ignoring the Center

Having an adequate command of the center is a life-and-death matter for Black. What happens if he ignores the center is well illustrated in the following opening:

WHITE	BLACK		WHITE	BLACK
1 P—Q4	P—KN3?		2 P—K4	B—N2

Black's fianchetto of his King Bishop is premature. His poor timing has allowed White an overwhelming Pawn center.

3 N—QB3	P—Q3		5 B—QB4	P—K3?
4 N—B3	N—Q2?		6 Castles	N—K2?

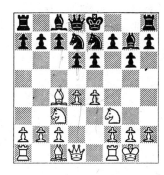

65

The Black pieces have no striking power.

Any expert player would dismiss Black's position as lost.

White has complete control of the center, while Black has neither center Pawn on the fourth rank.

White's Knights, are developed aggressively on the third rank; Black's Knights go timidly to the second rank.

Black's fianchettoed King Bishop accomplishes nothing, while his other Bishop is already destined to be a "problem child." White's Bishops, on the other hand, will have bold, free diagonals.

The Dangers of a Planless Opening

Sometimes Black's positional blunders are not so gross, and therefore perhaps not so easily recognizable; yet the results are equally disastrous. In the following example, Black's hit-or-miss development ruins his prospects.

WHITE	BLACK		WHITE	BLACK
1 P—K4	P—QN3?		2 P—Q4	B—N2

Black has made the same kind of mistake as in the previous example.

3 B—Q3	P—K3	4 N—KR3	....

Usually it is not good play to develop a Knight *away* from the center. Here the move is good because it prepares for the line-opening advance of White's King Bishop Pawn.

4	P—Q4	5 P—K5!	....

Black has belatedly advanced in the center, but White's reply creates difficulties for Black: he can no longer play ... N—KB3.

5	N—K2	7 P—KB4!	B—K2
6 Castles	N—N3	8 P—B5!	....

Black has had to develop his King-side pieces ineffectually, and his Queen Bishop has no scope. His position offers no promise whatever, and he will soon be exposed to a violent attack by White's well-placed forces. Since Black's pieces are not very active, his chances of successful resistance are microscopic.

These three samples of poor play can therefore serve as horrible examples of what Black must avoid in the opening. He need not find the *ideal development* or the *very best moves*. But he does need moves that give him a fighting chance, a basis for planning, a hope that he will have something to say about how the game unfolds. If he can achieve these substantial goals, he can truly say that he knows how to play the Black pieces.

5. PLAYING WITH AN ADVANTAGE IN MATERIAL

The Power of Pawn Promotion

HAVE YOU ever stopped to think that the strongest move on the chessboard—aside from actual checkmate—is the successful queening of a Pawn?

To obtain a new Queen so cheaply is the equivalent of winning your opponent's Queen!

If we think of Pawn promotion in this way, we can understand why the advantage of a Pawn plays such a big role in the games of the masters, and why it should play just as important a part in our own games.

In the two following diagrams we see how Pawn promotion "makes all the difference":

66

WHITE TO MOVE

At this moment White is "hopelessly" behind in material. Without the possibility of queening, he could safely resign. However, he plays 1 P—K8/Qch.

67

BLACK TO MOVE

Black is in check from the new Queen. He must move his King out of check. When he does so, White remorselessly continues 2 QxR, followed by checkmate.

Sometimes, it is true, the newly established Queen is immediately captured. But if there is a recapturing force at hand, the Pawn promotion still turns out to be highly profitable.

An example of material gain by Pawn promotion:

68

WHITE TO MOVE

White plays 1 P—B8/Q. As Black cannot afford to remain a Queen down, he plays 1 . . . RxQ. White of course replies 2 RxRch.

69

BLACK TO MOVE

Black has been able to get rid of the new Queen, but he has had to part with his Rook in the process. White has won a Rook!

The promotion of a Pawn is generally of decisive effect. Note, for example, how the newly created Queen took an active role in the position of Diagram 15. Diagrams 18 and 19 illustrate the same point.

70

WHITE TO MOVE

White plays 1 R—Q8. This is a very common maneuver with a Pawn that is already on the seventh rank, and you will find it very effective. The advanced White Rook blocks off Black's forces from the White Pawn.

71

BLACK TO MOVE

Black can resign. If he takes the White Rook, the passed Pawn recaptures, becoming a Queen. If Black refrains from capturing, the Pawn advances anyway, becomes a Queen, and is safe from recapture.

The all-important Pawn

A Knight or a Bishop cannot force checkmate. Therefore, if you are left with King and Knight (or King and Bishop) against a lone King, you cannot win.

But if the Bishop or Knight is assisted by only a single Pawn, then that Pawn, supported by the other forces, advances to the queening square.

72

WHITE TO MOVE

Without the lone White Pawn this position would be a draw. As matters stand, there follows 1 K—N4, K— K3; 2 KxP and then 3 KxP. The White Pawn will then advance to the eighth rank and become a Queen.

The examples in this chapter have shown the tremendous power of Pawn promotion.

However, we must not jump to the conclusion that Pawn promotion is easy to carry out or that it is appropriate in all parts of the game.

Pawn promotion is very rare in the opening, as it takes quite a few moves for a Pawn to reach the eighth rank. And, since there are a great many pieces on the board during the opening stage, the chances of the Pawn's reaching the last rank are slim indeed.

In the middle game the Pawn's promotion chances are somewhat brighter, but here too the game is complicated by various factors, such as attacking play against the King.

It is in the endgame stage, when the Queens have generally disappeared and when relatively few pieces are left on the board, that Pawn promotion begins to take the center of the stage.

It is in these rather simplified endgame positions, too, that the Kings can at last venture out to the center of the board, no longer terrified by the brutal attacking possibilities of the major pieces.

The new mobility of the Kings at this simplified stage reminds us that endings with only the Kings and Pawns on the board are the simplest kind of endings and therefore the logical ones to study first. So we now turn to them.

King and Pawn Endings

IN ONE SENSE, King and Pawn endings are very simple.

The material on the board has been greatly simplified. Only Kings and Pawns remain. Everything else has been swapped off.

However, King and Pawn endings abound in interesting finesses. In that sense, they are far from simple.

We need to be familiar with King and Pawn endings because some of them, as you will soon see, are of a standard form that is always a win.

This means that whenever you can manage to win a Pawn free and clear, you are in effect threatening to swap off all the pieces, reducing the game to a standard King and Pawn ending that is an almost automatic win for you! The threat of this simplification is a potent weapon in your handling of the game.

Passed Pawns

Most King and Pawn play revolves about passed Pawns—their creation and their advance to the queening square. (A passed Pawn is one that is not impeded by hostile Pawns on either of the neighboring files. In Diagrams 73 and 74, White has two passed Pawns.)

Some passed Pawns are especially powerful. We can see this in Diagrams 73 and 74.

73

CONNECTED PASSED PAWNS

White's passed Pawns are connected: they are placed on neighboring files. They are capable of protecting each other without their King's help.

Here is a typical line of play which wins for White in Diagram 21:

1 P—N6   K—B3

If 1 . . . KxP; 2 P—N7 and the Pawn cannot be prevented from queening.

2 K—B4	K—K2	5 P—B7ch	K—B1
3 K—K5	K—B1	6 K—K6	K—N2
4 P—B6	K—N1	7 K—K7	. . . .

White's King guards the queening square, so that he can now continue with 8 P—B8/Qch with a quick mate in the offing.

74

REMOTE PASSED PAWNS

Here White's Pawns are said to be "remote passed Pawns" or "distant passed Pawns." We use this term because they are too far away from the Black King to be caught by him as they advance to queen.

In Diagram 74 White's remote passed Pawns are so power-ful that White can queen a Pawn without the help of his King. This is how he does it:

$$1 \text{ P—N6} \qquad \dots$$

(White can also start the same process with 1 P—B6.)

$$1 \dots \qquad \text{K—B3}$$

For the moment the Black King can still catch either Pawn in time.

$$2 \text{ P—B6} \qquad \text{K—K3}$$

Else the Bishop Pawn marches through to promotion.

3 P—B7 K—Q2   4 P—N7   ....

Now it is too late for the Black King to catch the Knight Pawn, which will become a Queen on the next move.

75

WHITE TO MOVE
White's remote passed Pawn wins for him without the aid of his King.

In Diagram 75 the play is:

| 1 P—R4! | K—N2 | 3 P—R6 | K—K2 |
| 2 P—R5 | K—B2 | 4 P—R7 | K—Q2 |

And now White plays 5 P—R8/Q and will soon force checkmate. Thus we see from these examples the enormous power of the remote passed Pawn.

Now we come to a basic concept in chess known as the "Opposition." See Diagram 76.

76

WHITE TO MOVE

The Kings are in "Opposition." We use this term when they face each other with an odd number of squares between them. The King that does NOT have to move is said to "have the Opposition."

Before we see what happens in Diagram 76, please study the caption carefully. In the basic King and Pawn endings, which we are now about to study, the winning process often depends on "having the Opposition."

To make our study of Diagram 76 easier, let's assume for the moment that it's Black's turn to move: he plays 1 . . . P—QR4 and White replies 2 P—R4!

Now Black's Pawn moves are exhausted, and he has to move his King. That means that White has the Opposition—Black's King has to give way.

Why is this important to us?

Well, White is a Pawn ahead to begin with. He has a passed King Pawn which is momentarily blocked. If a free path is created for this passed Pawn, White can advance it, supported by its King, to the queening square.

Not only that; if Black's King gives way, White can advance his own King to Queen 5, capturing both weak Bishop Pawns. Here is what happens:

2	K—K2	4 KxP/B5	K—K3
3 K—Q5!	K—Q2	5 K—Q4!	. . . .

Now Black must move his King away from the King Pawn, allowing White to play 6 KxP. Then White is three Pawns up, and he has a new passed Pawn—the Bishop Pawn. By advancing both of his passed Pawns, supported by his King, White must promote to a Queen, leading up to a quick checkmate.

So far all this is clear and convincing, but remember we said in the caption to Diagram 76 that *White moves first.* Given that condition, White must be on the alert. For example, suppose he starts from Diagram 76 like this:

1 P—R4??   P—R4!

Now White has botched it. He has no Pawn moves, and must move his King. In other words, BLACK HAS THE OPPOSITION!

The consequence? After White moves his King, he loses his King Pawn, and the position is a draw!

Now back to Diagram 76. White *can* win, and this is how:

1 P—R3!!   P—R4   2 P—R4!!   . . . .

Note the finesse in making two moves with the Rook Pawn instead of one. Now it is White who after all has the Opposition; Black's King must give way; White plays 3 K—Q5, as shown above, and continues on his way to victory.

This was what we meant when we said that the simple King and Pawn endings are not always "simple." However, their tricky qualities add to their fascination.

77

WHO MOVES?

If Black moves, White wins. If White moves, the position is a draw. In other words: if White has the Opposition, he wins. If Black has the Opposition, he draws.

Diagram 77 is one of the most important situations in basic King and Pawn endings.

If Black moves, here is what happens:

1	K—Q1	2 P—Q7	K—K2
3 K—B7	....		

And on the next move White plays 4 P—Q8/Q, checkmating quickly.

If White moves first, he cannot win:

$$1 \text{ P—Q7ch} \qquad \text{K—Q1}$$

Now the only move to hold the Pawn is 2 K—Q6, but that causes stalemate!

Suppose White tries a different way:

1 K—N6	K—Q2	2 K—B5	K—Q1!
3 K—B6	K—B1		

Black has maneuvered his King to keep the Opposition. He thus maintains the draw.

The important moral is, then, that in the basic ending of King and Pawn vs. King, *you must make sure that you keep the Opposition.* The method will be explained in later endings.

78

WHITE TO MOVE

Here too White has stalemate troubles. Thus, if 1 K—B5, K—R1; 2 K—B6 and Black is stalemated. How is White to win?

In Diagram 78 White has more material than he needs for winning purposes. Here is how he solves his difficulty, getting rid of the stalemate:

1 P—R8/Qch!   KxQ   2 K—R6!   ....

The point. White has the Opposition. Black's King must give way.

2 ....   K—N1   3 P—N7   ....

Here is a valuable hint about positions where the stronger side's King does not control the queening square: whenever your Pawn advances to the seventh rank *without giving check*, you win the ending.

Black must now play 3 . . . K—B2, whereupon White continues 4 K—R7, making 5 P—N8/Q possible, followed by a quick mate.

79

WHO MOVES FIRST?

It doesn't matter! Because White's Pawn is still on the fifth rank, he can always advance the Pawn at any point where he has lost the Opposition. This will cause Black to give way with his King.

Suppose, in Diagram 27, that Black moves first. Then he has lost the Opposition, and his King must give way:

1 ....   K—Q1   2 K—B7   ....

(Or 1 . . . K—B1; 2 K—Q7 with the same result.)

| 2 .... | K—Q2 | 3 P—K6ch | K—Q1 |

Now White continues 4 P—K7ch followed by 5 P—K8/Q, followed by a quick checkmate.

Now back to Diagram 79. Suppose White moves first? What follows is extremely important, and you must study it until you fully understand it.

White must move his King, and therefore loses the Opposition:

$$1 \text{ K—Q6} \qquad ....$$

(Note that 1 K—B6 serves the same purpose.)

$$1 .... \qquad \text{K—Q1}$$

Black maintains the Opposition. So far so good for Black. But now White has a move in reserve:

$$2 \text{ P—K6!} \qquad ....$$

(In Diagram 77, White's Pawn was already on the sixth rank, so he no longer had this "tempo" move in reserve!)

$$2 .... \qquad \text{K—K1}$$

Black's King must give way. He has lost the Opposition.

$$3 \text{ P—K7} \qquad ....$$

The Pawn has advanced to the seventh rank *without check*.

As we know from earlier examples, this means that White's Pawn will soon become a Queen and enforce checkmate.

An important moral we deduce from Diagram 79 is this: if your single Pawn has not reached the sixth rank, don't advance it too hastily. Reserve the moves of the Pawn to a time when you will be badly in need of them.

Now let's apply what we've learned.

80

WHO MOVES FIRST?

It doesn't matter. If Black moves first, he loses the Opposition immediately, and White wins with ease. If White moves first, he keeps the Opposition with the tempo move 1 P—Q4!

Diagram 80 should offer no difficulties.

If Black moves first, White quickly lays down a path for his Pawn to advance and queen. For example:

1	K—K2	3 K—Q6	K—B1
2 K—B6!	K—Q1	4 P—Q4	K—Q1
	5 P—Q5	....	

Again Black loses the Opposition: 5 . . . K—K1; 6 K—B7 etc. or 5 . . . K—B1; 6 K—K7 etc. and White's King guards the queening square.

If White moves first in Diagram 80, the procedure is pretty much the same:

1 P—Q4!	K—K2	4 K—B7	K—K2
2 K—B6	K—Q1	5 P—Q5	K—K1
3 K—Q6	K—K1	6 P—Q6	K—B1
	7 P—Q7	....	

Again the Pawn becomes a Queen and forces checkmate.

There is still one more vital point we need to know about King and Pawn endings.

In Diagram 80 White's King was ideally posted—*in front of the Pawn*. However, if the stronger side's King is at the side of the Pawn, or in back of it, and if the weaker side's King is well advanced, the lone King can draw.

81

BLACK DRAWS!

Black is able to draw because, due to the unfavorable position of the White King, Black can always assume the Opposition at the critical moment.

Diagram 81 is a draw no matter who moves first.

Let's see the play with Black moving first. He loses the Opposition at once, but he regains it when he needs it. This will lead in due course to the drawing method of Diagram 77.

| 1 .... | K—Q4 | 2 P—Q4 | K—Q3! |

After 2 . . . K—B5??; 3 K—K4! White wins because Black can never get back the Opposition. (If 3 . . . K—N4; 4 K—Q5!)

| 3 K—K4 | K—K3! | 5 K—Q4 | K—Q2 |
| 4 P—Q5ch | K—Q3 | 6 K—K5 | K—K2! |

If 6 . . . K—B2??; 7 K—K6 and White gets the Opposition after 7 . . . K—Q1; 8 K—Q6. Then if 8 . . . K—K1; 9 K—B7 wins; or 8 . . . K—B1; 9 K—K7 wins in familiar fashion.

| 7 P—Q6ch | K—Q2 | 8 K—Q5 | .... |

A crucial situation for Black. If 8 . . . K—B1??; 9 K—B6 White gains the Opposition and wins. The same thing happens after 8 . . . K—K1??; 9 K—K6.

But Black does have a saving move:

8 ....   K—Q1!!   9 K—B6   ....

Or 9 K—K6, K—K1 with a similar windup.

9 ....   K—B1!

Now we have the exact position of Diagram 77 with Black having the Opposition and White having to move. As we know from Diagram 77, this is a drawn position.

From our study of the positions in this chapter, you now know which positions to aim for when a King and Pawn ending is in prospect, and which positions to avoid.

You have learned of the importance of the Opposition, and you have seen how you can use it to your advantage by keeping Pawn moves in reserve.

These positions are well worth playing over, preferably with a friend, so that you can iron out any misunderstandings. You will find that familiarity with these endings is very profitable in terms of additional wins you will score.

How to Simplify into a Won Ending

SIMPLIFYING has two aspects.

The player who is ahead in material wants a placid game without complications, so that he can proceed to make use of his extra material without being disturbed by side-issues.

The player who has a material disadvantage naturally avoids simplifying as much as he can, and, just as naturally, seeks complications. The simpler the position, the more assured is his ultimate defeat. Complications, tricks, confusion offer him his best practical chance.

But this is not the only conflict on simplification.

The player who has a material advantage wants to simplify by exchanging *pieces*, particularly the Queen. (The Queen is the great troublemaker in such situations; its long-range potentialities can often stir up an unwelcome surprise.)

However, this same player is opposed to exchanging *Pawns*. We noticed this in a number of earlier endings. His opposition is based on two points.

First, he needs Pawns as queening candidates. (Just think of Diagram 72 in this respect.) The more Pawns he retains, the better his queening chances.

Don't interpret this point too literally. It does not call for a slavish avoidance of all Pawn exchanges; it merely emphasizes the need for caution.

As for the player who is behind in material, he avoids the exchange of pieces if he can, but seeks the exchange of Pawns where he can do so.

Removing the Queens

Now let's see some illustrations of how the exchange of Queens is brought about in actual play.

82

WHITE TO MOVE

White is a Pawn ahead and is naturally eager to exchange Queens. This is accomplished directly by a Queen check: 1 Q—K4ch. Whether Black exchanges or allows White to exchange, the Queens disappear.

In Diagram 83 a check again has the desired effect.

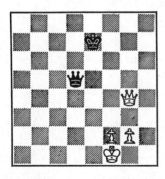

83

BLACK TO MOVE

White is two Pawns ahead but he must look forward to a long series of checks. Luckily, when Black tries 1 . . . Q—N4ch White has 2 Q—K2ch! forcing a King and Pawn ending which is effortlessly won for White.

In Diagram 84 Black's immediate resignation comes as something of a surprise.

84

BLACK TO MOVE

Though White is a Pawn ahead, it does not seem possible for him to maintain this advantage or turn it to use. Also, the position is so open that Black's chances of perpetual check are very promising.

Yet Black's resignation is quite in order, as we can see from the following play:

1 ....   K—B2

(Or any other King move to the second rank.)

2 Q—Q7ch!   ....

If Black's King goes to the third rank, then 3 Q—Q6ch! forces the exchange of Queens. In that event White's King wins the remaining Black Pawn and advances his own Knight Pawn to queen. Meanwhile Black's King is held in a vise by the White Rook Pawn.

2 ....   K—N1

On 2 ... K—B1 White has 3 Q—Q6ch! and on 2 ... K—R1 White wins as in the text.

3 Q—B8ch!   K—B2

It doesn't matter where the Black King goes.

4 Q—N7ch!   ....

Forcing the easily won King and Pawn ending described in the note to White's second move.

This is a fine example of simplifying technique.

Of course, it isn't always necessary to have a check available to force a simplified position. Any other kind of strong threat can do the trick.

85

WHITE TO MOVE

White is a Pawn ahead and would therefore like to exchange Queens. He doesn't have a check at his disposal, but 1 Q—Q6! does equally well. As Black's Rook is threatened, he has nothing better than 1 . . . QxQ; 2 RxQ. Thus White has achieved his objective.

In Diagram 86, too, White does not have a check but he has an equally effective threat.

86

BLACK TO MOVE

White is a Pawn ahead. In addition, he has an overwhelming position, in view of the mating threat Q—K7. Thus he forces Black to seek the exchange of Queens even though Black is already behind in material.

1	Q—B8ch

Or 1 . . . Q—K1; 2 QxQ, RxQ; 3 R—Q6 winning a second Pawn for White.

2 K—N2	Q—B5	3 QxQ	PxQ
	4 R—QB7	....	

Winning a second Pawn anyway.

| 4 .... | R—QN1 | | 5 RxBP | R—N3 |
| | 6 R—B7 | R—N7 | | |

If Black's Rook stays on the third rank, White wins by
advancing his King-side Pawns, escorted by their King.

7 R—B6	RxRP		12 P—B3	P—QR4
8 RxBP	K—N2		13 P—R4	P—R3
9 R—QN6	R—R4		14 P—N5	P—R4
10 P—N4	R—R5		15 P—B5	R—R8
11 K—N3	R—R6ch		16 R—N7ch	Resigns

White's Pawns advance irresistibly.

In Diagram 87 we see a whole arsenal of threats used by
White to force a favorable ending and then win it.

87

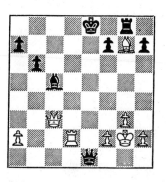

BLACK TO MOVE

*Momentarily material is even. How-
ever, White has the nasty threat of
R—Q8ch winning Black's Queen. If
Black tries 1 ... Q—K5ch; 2 P—B3,
Q—K6; 3 B—B6!! wins. And if 1
... Q—K3; 2 Q—Q3! is decisive.*

Because of the variations shown in the caption to Diagram
87, Black decides to give up the Queen.

| 1 .... | RxB | | 2 R—Q8ch! | KxR |
| | 3 QxQ | .... | | |

The Queen is definitely stronger than the Rook and Bishop.
The play that follows is a wonderful example of the power
of the Queen.

White's immediate threat is 4 Q—K5! attacking the Rook. If then 4 . . . R—N3; 5 Q—R8ch wins a Pawn, likewise after 4 . . . B—B1; 5 Q—N8ch. Finally, if 4 . . . R—N1?; 5 Q—N8ch wins the Rook.

| 3 . . . . | R—N3 | 4 Q—K4! | . . . . |

Threatening to win the Queen Rook Pawn with 5 Q—R8ch or the King Rook Pawn with 5 Q—R4ch.

Black must lose one Pawn or the other. Which one is he to preserve? The King Rook Pawn, for if he loses it, White gets a *passed Pawn* at once. This passed Pawn will at once advance—a candidate for queening.

| 4 . . . . | P—KR3 | 6 QxPch | K—B1 |
| 5 Q—R8ch | K—K2 | 7 P—QR4! | . . . . |

A clever move. White threatens 8 P—R5 when Black's Pawn cannot recapture because of the pin. The sequel would be 9 P—R6, with a dangerous passed Pawn that would queen quickly.

| 7 . . . . | B—N5 | 9 Q—K5ch | K—N1 |
| 8 Q—N8ch | K—N2 | 10 P—B4 | . . . . |

A good move which undermines the position of Black's Rook on the third rank because of the possibility of P—B5.

| 10 . . . . | R—K3 | 11 Q—QN5 | B—B1 |

Note that 11 . . . B—B4? is all wrong because of 11 P—R5! and 12 P—R6 with a winning passed Pawn.

| 12 P—B5 | R—Q3 | 13 K—B3! | . . . . |

White brings his King to the Queen-side. He intends to win the Knight Pawn.

| 13 .... | R—Q5 | 14 K—K3! | .... |

To exchange Pawns by 14 QxP?, RxP would run counter to the great principle of avoiding Pawn exchanges. This capture would make White's victory extremely difficult.

| 14 .... | R—QN5 |

If instead 14 . . . B—B4; 15 Q—K8ch, K—N2 (he must guard his Bishop Pawn); 16 Q—K5ch and 17 QxR! with an easy win in the King and Pawn ending.

| 15 Q—K8 | K—N2 | 16 K—Q3 | K—N1 |
| | 17 K—B3 | .... | |

Threatening to force a won King and Pawn ending with 18 QxBch!, KxQ; 19 KxR etc.

| 17 .... | R—N5 |

He tries to keep White's King from crossing the fourth rank. Thus, if 17 . . . R—N8; 18 K—B4, R—N5ch; 19 K—Q5, R—N7; 20 K—B6 when White keeps the Knight Pawn under attack and advances his King-side Pawns against Black's weakened forces.

| 18 Q—N5 | B—B4 |

The game is reaching the decisive point.

| 19 K—N3! | .... |

Now Black is lost.

Thus, if 19 . . . R—N5ch; 20 QxR, BxQ; 21 KxB with a won King and Pawn ending.

And if 19 . . . B—Q5; 20 P—B6! (threatening 21 Q—K8ch and 22 QxPch). After 20 . . . BxP White wins easily because of the passed Queen Rook Pawn he gets by 21 QxP.

So Black has nothing better than 20 . . . K—R2. But then

21 Q—B5ch, R—N3; 22 Q—Q7!, BxP; 23 QxPch, B—N2;
24 Q—B5! is decisive.

19 . . . .   K—N2   20 P—R5!   Resigns

For if 20 . . . R—N5ch; 21 QxR, BxQ and now 22 P—
R6! forces the queening of the Queen Rook Pawn!

A very fine ending, played in masterly style by White.

In Diagram 88 an extremely subtle maneuver wins for
White.

88

WHITE TO MOVE

*The most obvious continuation, since
White is a Pawn up, is to exchange
the Queens and Rooks. But in that
case White cannot win!*

If White plays 1 QxQch, KxQ; 2 RxRch, KxR the simplification turns out to be faulty because White's King is
tied down by Black's passed Queen Rook Pawn. The White
King-side Pawns cannot win by themselves, and thus White
is held to a draw.

Yet White can win with a subtle waiting move:

1 Q—N6!!   . . . .

Now Black cannot play 1 . . . K—B1?? because of 2 R—
N8 mate.

Nor can he play 1 . . . Q—Q2?? because of 2 R—N8ch,
K—K2; 3 Q—N5ch and mate next move.

Nor can Black play his Queen further afield because of
the reply QxPch.

Therefore Black can only move a Pawn.

If he plays 1 . . . P—R5 then 2 K—B1! If now 2 . . . P—R6 White exchanges all the pieces then plays K—N1—R2 capturing the Rook Pawn and then winning easily by playing K—N4—B5—Q6 etc.

And if Black plays 2 . . . Q—R6ch, White wins with 3 K—N1!, Q—K2; 4 K—R2, P—R6 (forced!); 5 QxRch etc. again winning the Rook Pawn.

| 1 .... | P—N5 | 2 PxP | PxP |

Or 2 . . . QxPch; 3 K—K2!, Q—K2; 4 QxRch, QxQ; 5 RxQ, KxR; 6 K—Q2, K—N3; 7 K—B3, followed by K—N2—R3—R4 and KxP winning easily.

| 3 K—Q1! | Resigns |

Black gives up because if 3 . . . P—N6; 4 PxP, PxP and now White exchanges pieces followed by 5 K—B1—N2 and KxP.

Or if 3 . . . P—B6; 4 QxRch, QxQ; 5 RxQ, KxR; 6 K—B1 followed by K—N1—R2—N3 and KxP. As already shown, White can then liquidate the Queen-side Pawns and bring his King to the King-side to aid the queening of his Pawns there.

In Diagram 89 White wins by a series of delightful finesses.

89

WHITE TO MOVE

White is a Pawn up but he cannot make any headway in the Rook and Pawn ending. He therefore decides on the maneuver R—K6 followed by R—K5 forcing a won King and Pawn ending.

| 1 R—K6! | K—Q2 | 2 R—K5! | RxR |
| | 3 PxR | .... | |

If now 3 . . . K—K3; 4 K—Q4, K—K2; 5 K—Q5, K—Q2; 6 P—K6ch, K—K2; 7 K—K5 followed by 8 KxP and White wins as he pleases.

| | 3 .... | K—K2! |

Setting a sly trap.

If now 4 K—Q4, K—K3! and White cannot win.

For example 5 P—K4?, P—B5! and Black wins the advanced Pawn.

Or if 5 K—B5, KxP; 6 KxP, K—K5; 7 KxP, KxP; 8 P—N4, P—B5. Both players get new Queens and the ending is drawn.

| | 4 K—Q3!! | .... |

Now if 4 . . . K—K3; 5 K—Q4 wins as shown in the note to White's third move.

| 4 .... | K—Q2 | 5 P—K4!! | .... |

So that if 5 . . . PxPch; 6 KxP, K—K3; 7 K—Q4, K—K2; 8 K—B5 and White gives up his King Pawn to win both Black Pawns with an easy victory in sight.

| 5 .... | P—B5! | 6 K—K2!! | K—K3 |

Black's last hope. After the natural reply 7 K—B3??, KxP White loses!

| 7 K—B2!! | KxP | 7 K—B3 | Resigns |

For he must move his King, allowing 8 KxP with an easy win for White.

An exciting and beautiful ending.

Diagram 90 shows a skillful transition to a won King and Pawn ending.

90

BLACK TO MOVE

*Material is even, but Black can force
a won King and Pawn ending.*

Black's first move is the key to the win:

| 1 .... | R—B8ch!! | 3 KxR | KxR |
| 2 RxR | RxRch | 4 K—Q2 | K—N7 |

Black now continues, no matter how White plays, with . . .
K—N6 and . . . KxP. This gives him a won King and Pawn
ending.

In this section you have seen how to simplify into an endgame where you can utilize a material advantage successfully.
To sum up, the chief methods of simplifying are: (1) exchanging Queens; (2) using tactical threats; (3) forcing
weaknesses in the hostile position; (4) relying on accurate
timing.

6. BRILLIANT COMBINATIONS AND SACRIFICES

We all enjoy playing over brilliant combinations. They give us thrills that cannot be equalled by any other aspect of the game. It would give us even greater pleasure to make such brilliant plays in our own games. But many of us feel that these combinations are a matter of inspiration, and hence the exclusive property of the masters and other first-rate players.

Actually, this is not so, for brilliant play can be studied and mastered, just like any other aspect of chess. The important thing to remember is that these strokes of brilliancy are made possible by definite patterns and themes of tactical play. Once you have become familiar enough with these themes to use them in your own games, you are equipped to play brilliant chess.

In this chapter you have a chance to study a great many examples of the four themes that are most frequently encountered in actual play. The diagrams and solutions will do more than add to your knowledge. They will also delight you by showing you some of the most beautiful moves ever played on the chessboard.

The *pin* is by far the most frequently used tactical theme. In Diagram 91 Black's Queen is "pinned"—it cannot move off the diagonal leading to the Black King. Hence White can exploit the helplessness of Black's Queen by a very brilliant move.

The next most common theme is the *Knight fork*. Actually, this is a special case of the double attack, but it is particularly effective and particularly dreaded (especially by inexperienced players). It turns up in Diagram 104, and involves a simultaneous attack by a Knight on two or more enemy units. The task in Diagram 104 is to move the White Knight in such a way that it will fork Black's Queen and Rook.

If you are unfamiliar with this theme, the chances are that you will never see the simple yet subtle move that makes the Knight fork possible. On the other hand, if you *are* familiar with the theme, you will see in a flash what is the necessary preliminary move.

Discovered attack is one of the most common, as well as one of the most potent, combination themes. It is well illustrated in Diagram 109, where White makes a discovered attack on the hostile Bishop and at the same time unleashes a mating threat on another part of the board. The simultaneous nature of the attack makes it very difficult to parry. (Note, by the way, that the word "discovered" as used here really means "uncovered.")

Another frequently used and powerful technique is the *double attack*. This type of attack—*simultaneous attack by a single unit on two hostile units*—is the very essence of chess. This attack is economical and profitable. It appeals to the player who knows how to get the maximum effect from his pieces.

A good example of this technique is Diagram 113 in which White attacks the advanced Black Bishop a second time and also threatens mate. Black cannot parry both threats; consequently he loses his Bishop.

Once you have familiarized yourself with these themes your play will be enormously strengthened. For these themes are more than concepts; they are weapons. Using these weapons has a cumulative value: the more often you use them, the more skillful you become in applying them. Thus every present success in using them promises a future, even more successful, use of them in your games to come.

White Moves First

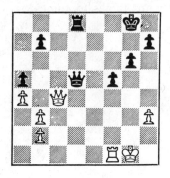

91

92

93

94

91 PIN

White exploits the pin on Black's Queen by:

1	R—Q1!	QxQ
2	RxRch!	K any
3	PxQ	. . . .

White has won a Rook.

92 PIN

White profits by the position of his Rook on the open King Bishop file:

1	BxN!	QxB
2	QxQ	PxQ
3	BxB	. . . .

And Black cannot retake.

93 PIN

White cuts off the protection of Black's pinned Bishop by Black's Queen:

1	N—K6!	. . . .

Black has no satisfactory defense to the threat of 2 QxB mate.

94 PIN

White exploits his opponent's vulnerable set-up on the Queen file:

1	P—B4!	N—K2

If 1 . . . NxP; 2 RxN.

2	P—B5	. . . .

White wins a piece.

White Moves First

95

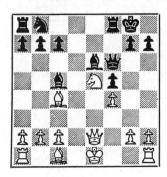

96

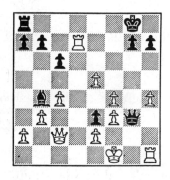

97

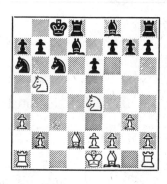

98

95 PIN

White undermines Black's advanced Black Knight by:

| 1 P—KN4! | B—N3 |
| 2 NxB | . . . . |

Now that the Knight's protection is gone, White wins a piece.

96 PIN

Double attack reinforces White's pin:

| 1 N—Q7! | NxN |
| 2 QxBch | R—B2 |

Forced, otherwise Black loses the Knight.

| 3 QxRch | QxQ |
| 4 BxQch | . . . . |

White has won the Exchange.

97 PIN

How does White meet the mate threat?

| 1 RxPch! | KxR |

White answers 1 . . . QxR with the same move.

| 2 R—N1 | . . . . |

White wins the Queen.

98 KNIGHT FORK

1 N—Q6ch	BxN
2 NxBch	K any
3 NxBP	. . . ..

White wins a Pawn and the Exchange.

White Moves First

99

100

101

102

99 KNIGHT FORK

	1 N—B7ch!	K—K2

Or 1 . . . RxN, losing the Exchange.

2 RxR	RxR
3 RxR	KxR
4 N—K6ch	. . . .

White wins the Bishop.

100 KNIGHT FORK

White combines a fork and a pin:

1 RxRch	RxR
2 RxRch	QxR
3 NxPch	. . . .

Winning the Queen.

101 KNIGHT FORK

	1 N—Q6	. . . .

Threatens NxBch and also N—B5ch.

1	B—Q2
2 R—K7ch	K—B3
3 RxB	K—K3
4 R—Q8	K—K2
5 N—B5ch	. . . .

White remains a piece ahead as a result of this fork.

102 KNIGHT FORK

1 NxQP	BxN
2 N—Q7ch	. . . .

White wins the Queen. (Another way is 1 N—Q7ch, BxN; 2 NxP winning the Queen because of the threatened 3 Q—R8 mate.)

White Moves First

103

104

105

106

103 KNIGHT FORK

1 Q—R8ch!	K—R2
2 N—B3	....

White made room for the Knight fork, which wins the Exchange.

104 KNIGHT FORK

1 N—R6ch	K—R1
2 QxB!	....

The subtle preparation for a Knight fork.

2	QxQ
3 NxPch!	....

This fork cannot be answered by 3 . . . RxN, because of 4 R—Q8ch forcing mate.

3	K—N1
4 NxQ	....

White has won a piece.

105 KNIGHT FORK

1 N—Q5!!	QxBP
2 RxNPch!	KxR
3 Q—N4ch	K—B1

Or 3 . . . K—R1; 4 N—B7 mate.

4 N—K7ch	....

The Knight fork wins Black's Queen.

106 DISCOVERED ATTACK

1 Q—N4	....

Threatening mate and indirectly menacing Black's Queen.

1	P—N3

Or 1 . . . P—B3 with the same result.

2 N—R6ch	....

Winning Black's Queen.

White Moves First

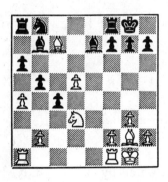

107

108

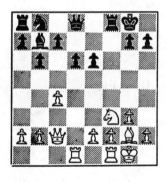

109

110

107 DISCOVERED ATTACK

1	P—Q6!	BxB
2	PxB	R—K1
3	KxB	PxN
4	PxP	RxP
5	P—N6!	....

White's far advanced Pawn assures him an easy win.

108 DISCOVERED ATTACK

1	NxB!	....

White leaves his Queen open to attack, yet he must win at least a piece. For example: 1 . . . RxQ; 2 Nx Qch and 3 RxR.

Or 1 . . . RxN; 2 QxR, etc.

109 DISCOVERED ATTACK

1	N—N5!	....

Threatens mate.

1	....	QxN
2	BxB	....

White wins the Exchange.

110 DISCOVERED ATTACK

1	NxN!	QxQ

If 1 . . . QxN/B3; 2 Q—N7 mate.

2	NxNch	K—R1
3	N—B7 mate	

White Moves First

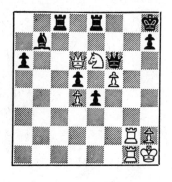

111

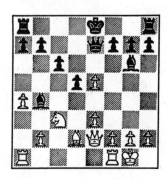

112

113

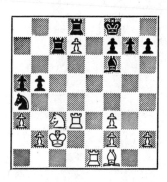

114

111 DISCOVERED ATTACK

       1 N—B8!!   RxN

If 1 . . . QxQ; 2 R—N8 mate.

If 1 . . . QxN; 2 R—N8ch forces mate.

       2 R—N8ch!   RxR

       3 QxQch   R—N2

       4 QxR mate

112 DOUBLE ATTACK

       1 NxP   PxN

       2 Q—N5ch   . . . .

White wins a Pawn.

113 DOUBLE ATTACK

       1 Q—K4

This wins a piece, as Black must guard against the threat of QxRP mate.

114 DOUBLE ATTACK

       1 R—K8ch   RxR

       2 PxR/Qch   KxQ

       3 R—K3ch!   . . . .

Black loses a piece however he plays. Thus, if 3 . . . B—K2 or 3 . . . R—K2 or 3 . . . K—Q2; 4 BxPch winning the Knight.

    And if 3 . . . K—B1 or 3 . . . K—Q1; 4 BxP wins the Knight because of the threatened 5 R—K8 mate.

White Moves First

115

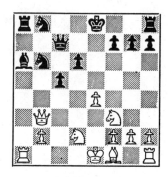

116

117

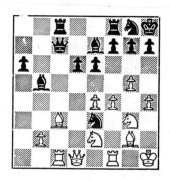

118

115 DOUBLE ATTACK

       1 B—K6!   ....

Black is lost.

For example: 1 . . . QBxB; 2 Q—B8ch forcing mate. Or 1 . . . RxR; 2 Q—K8 mate. Or 1 . . . PxB; 2 Q—R8ch forcing mate.

116 DOUBLE ATTACK

       1 BxB   RxB

Or 1 . . . NxB; 2 RxN! etc.

       2 RxR   NxR
       3 Q—N5ch   ....

White wins a piece.

117 DOUBLE ATTACK

       1 Q—B3ch   K moves
       2 Q—K1   ....

White wins the Rook or the Bishop.

118 DOUBLE ATTACK

Apparently Black is just on the point of winning the Exchange. However—

       1 Q—Q4   ....

This wins the Knight because of the mate threat.

Black Moves First

119

120

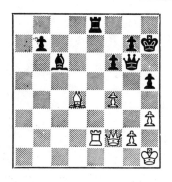

121

122

119 PIN

Black wins because of his pin on the White Knight.

1	NxP!
2 PxN	RxPch!
3 QxR	RxN mate

120 PIN

It would be pointless to play 1 . . . PxN? because of 2 QxNch. Therefore:

1	Q—K2!

(1 . . . R—K3 also wins, for if 2 Q—KB2, Q—K2; 3 N—Q2, R—K7.)

White's Knight is lost, for if 2 N—N3, PxNch.

121 PIN

1	QxPch!
2 QxQ	RxR

White has nothing better than 3 QxB, leaving him the Exchange and a Pawn down.

122 KNIGHT FORK

1	R—Q7!
2 QxR	. . . .

On other Queen moves, such as 2 Q—B1 or 2 Q—B3, Black plays 2 . . . QxKP threatening mate. This forces 3 QxR, after which Black wins as in the text.

2	N—B6ch

Black forks King and Queen.

Black Moves First

123

124

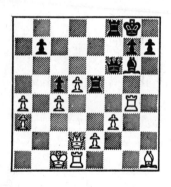

125

126

123 KNIGHT FORK

1	QxR!
2 RxQ	N—Q6ch
3 K any	NxQ

Black has won a Rook, and stands to win more material.

124 DISCOVERED ATTACK

1	N—B2

Black wins a piece, as he attacks the Bishop and Knight.

125 DISCOVERED ATTACK

1	RxKP!
2 QxR	Q—B6ch

And mate next move.

126 DISCOVERED ATTACK

1	NxP!

This wins a Pawn, for if 2 PxN, BxB. Or if 2 BxB, N—Q6ch.

Black Moves First

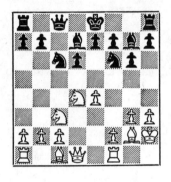

127

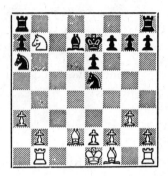

128

129

130

127 DISCOVERED ATTACK

1	....	NxN
2	QxN	N—N5ch!

Followed by 3 . . . BxQ and wins.

128 DOUBLE ATTACK

1	....	B—B3

Attacking Knight and Rook, and therefore winning at least a piece.

129 DOUBLE ATTACK

1	....	P—Q6!
2	RxP	RxR
3	QxR	P—K5
4	BxN	PxB!

Winning a piece.

130 DOUBLE ATTACK

1	....	QxQ
2	RxQ	B—N5
3	R/Q2—Q1	R—B7

Black wins a piece.

7. PRACTICAL CHECKMATES

THOUGH THERE are many aspects of chess that require study, the checkmate process remains the basic bit of knowledge required of every chess player.

Most players, although they need and would like to have more knowledge about checkmates, find that is unfortunately hard to come by. Most of the checkmate positions we ordinarily see are from made-up or composed problems. These often have elements of striking beauty, but they lack practical value. We do not see how they can be applied in our own games.

The diagrams and solutions in this chapter, however, show us checkmates taken from actual play. They are taken from situations that really happened in tournament play. That is what makes them so immensely valuable for us. When you have studied them and gained an understanding of these checkmates, you will be less at a loss on how to bring a game to a satisfactory end. Knowing these checkmates, then, is a step toward playing decisive chess with a clear goal before you.

All the checkmates described in this chapter have one outstanding feature in common. Regardless of whether the winner has a plus in material or not, he wins by some bright turn, some neat sequence. In other words, inspiration, rather than material advantage, is the keynote to many of these checkmates.

What has been accomplished once, can be accomplished repeatedly. Study, analyze, and understand these ingenious checkmates. When you know them well you will be able to apply these brilliant winning methods in your own games, and this will not only make you a better player but also increase your enjoyment of the game.

White Moves First

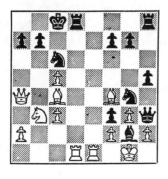

131

132

133

134

Solutions

131

1 QxNch	PxQ
2 B—QR6 mate	

132

1 Q—R6	PxQ
2 NxP mate	

133

1 QxNch	RxQ
2 R—Q8ch	Q—K1
3 RxQch	R—B1
4 RxR mate	

134

1 QxRch	KxQ
2 R—K8 mate	

White Moves First

135

136

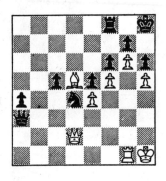

137

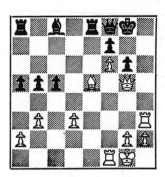

138

135

1 P—R8/Qch	RxQ
2 N—B5ch	K—N1
3 RxRch	KxR
4 Q—R6ch	any
5 Q—N7 mate	

136

1 Q—KR8ch	KxQ
2 P—N7ch	K—N1
3 B—R7ch	KxB
4 P—N8/Q mate	

137

1 QxPch	PxQ
2 P—N7ch	K—R2
3 PxR/Nch	K—R1
4 R—N8 mate	

138

1 QxPch	PxQ
2 P—B7ch	QxP
3 R—R8 mate	

White Moves First

139

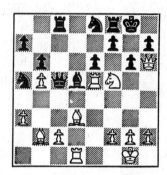

140

141

142

139

1 R—R8ch	KxR
2 R—R1ch	K—N1
3 R—R8ch	KxR
4 Q—R1ch	Q—R7
5 QxQch	K—N1
6 Q—R7 mate	

140

1 N—K7ch	QxN
2 QxRPch	KxQ
3 R—R5ch	K—N1
4 R—R8 mate	

141

1 N—K7ch	QxN
2 R—R8ch	KxR

Or 2 . . . K—B2; 3 Q—R5ch and mate next move.

3 Q—R5ch	K—N1
4 Q—R7ch	K—B2
5 B—N6 mate	

142

1 R—R8ch	BxR
2 RxBch	KxR
3 Q—R6ch	K—N1
4 N—B6 mate	

White Moves First

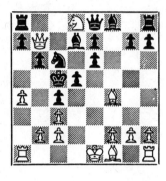

143

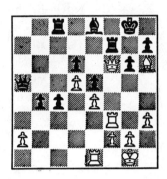

144

145

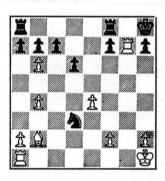

146

143

1 QxNch   BxQ
2 NxP mate

144

1 Q—K7   Q—B2
2 Q—B8ch   RxQ
3 RxR mate

145

1 R—B8ch   QxR
2 QxNPch   RxQ
3 RxR mate

146

1 R—N8 dbl ch   KxR
2 R—KN1 mate

White Moves First

147

148

149

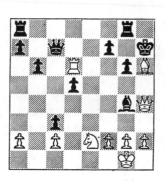

150

147

1	N—K7 dbl ch	K—R1
2	N—N6ch	PxN
3	RPxN dis ch	Q—R5
4	RxQ mate	

148

1	Q—Q7ch	BxQ
2	N—Q6 dis ch	K—Q1
3	N—B7ch	K—B1
4	R—K8ch	BxR
5	R—Q8 mate	

149

1	Q—Q8ch	KxQ
2	B—R5 dbl ch	K any
3	R—Q8 mate	

150

1	B—B8 dis ch	B—R4
2	QxBch	PxQ
3	R—R6 mate	

White Moves First

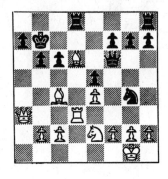

151

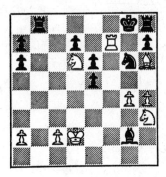

152

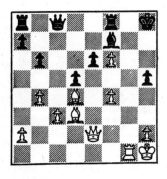

153

154

151

1 QxPch	KxQ
2 R—QR3ch	K—N2
3 B—R6ch	K—R2
4 B—QB8 mate	

152

1 R—N7ch	K—B1
2 RxQP dis ch	K—N1
3 R—KN7ch	K—B1
4 R—N7 dis ch	K—N1
5 RxRch	N—B1
6 RxN mate	

153

1 QxRPch	BxQ
2 P—B7 dis ch	P—K4
3 BxKP mate	

154

1 Q—R8ch	N—N1
2 QxPch	KxQ
3 BxB dis ch	K—R1
4 RxNch	KxR
5 R—N1ch	K—R1
6 B—B6 mate	

White Moves First

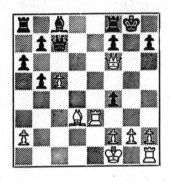

155

156

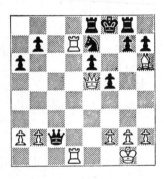

157

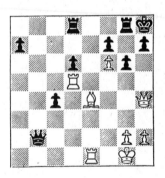

158

155

1 R—N3ch	PxR
2 BxPch	KxB
3 RPxR dis ch	B—R6
4 RxBch	K—N1
5 Q—R8 mate	

(Or 5 R—R8 mate or 5 Q—N5 mate.)

156

1 B—R7ch	K—R1
2 B—N8 dis ch	KxB

(Or 2 . . . B—R3; 3 Q—R7 mate.)

3 Q—R7 mate	

157

1 Q—B6 mate	

158

1 QxPch	KxQ
2 R—KR5 mate	

Black Moves First

159

160

161

162

Solutions

159

1	....	QxNch
2	RxQ	R—N8ch
3	Q—Q1	RxQch
4	R—B1	B—Q5ch
5	K—R1	RxR mate

160

1	....	QxPch
2	KxQ	R—R5ch
3	K—N1	R—R8ch
4	NxR	PxN/Q mate

161

1	....	Q—Q3ch
2	K—R3	N—B5ch
3	K—N3	N—R4 dbl ch
4	K—R3	Q—N6ch
5	RxQ	N—B5 mate

162

1	....	QxPch
2	NxQ	NxP mate

Black Moves First

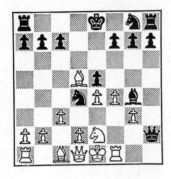

163

164

165

166

163

1	....	N—B7ch
2	QxN	QxN mate

164

1	....	R—K8ch
2	NxR	....

(Or 2 QxR, QxN mate.)

2	....	Q—R8 mate

165

1	....	Q—N7ch
2	KxQ	RxNP mate

166

1	....	N—B6 mate

Black Moves First

167

168

169

170

167

1	B—Q6 dbl ch
2 K—K1	R—B8 mate

168

1	N—R5 dis ch
2 K—K1	....

(Or 2 K—N1, Q—KN5 mate.)

2	NxN mate

169

1	R—KR3ch
2 K—N1	R—R8ch
3 KxR	Q—R6ch
4 K—N1	QxP(N7) mate

170

1	K—R2
2 B—K1	K—R3
3 B—B3	K—R4
4 B—K1	K—N5
5 B—B3	PxPch
6 RxPch	K—R6
7 any	BxR mate

8. A KEY TO THE OPENINGS

ALAPIN'S OPENING: 1 P—K4, P—K4; 2 N—K2

This is a poor opening for White because his Knight's development is not aggressive and because it blocks White's King Bishop. (See Diagram 40.)

ALBIN COUNTER GAMBIT: 1 P—Q4, P—Q4; 2 P—QB4, P—K4

Black's counter gambit is premature and unsound. After 3 QPxP, P—Q5 Black must rely on tricky play to compensate for his minus Pawn. White gets a clear advantage by straightforward development.

ALEKHINE'S DEFENSE: 1 P—K4, N—KB3

Black tempts the advance of White's center Pawns. After 2 P—K5, N—Q4; 3 P—QB4, N—N3; 4 P—Q4, P—Q3; 5 P—KB4 White has a formidable center and a tremendous advantage in mobility. With accurate play he can stifle Black. (See Diagram 26.)

BIRD'S OPENING: 1 P—KB4

This avoidance of a center Pawn move generally hampers White's development. White rarely plays this opening, which has remained a specialized resource of a small number of players.

BISHOP'S OPENING: 1 P—K4, P—K4; 2 B—B4

Old-fashioned and rarely played nowadays. The move of the Bishop lacks bite and White therefore generally plays 2 N—KB3.

BLUMENFELD COUNTER GAMBIT: 1 P—Q4, N—KB3; 2 N—KB3, P—K3; 3 P—B4, P—B4; 4 P—Q5, P—QN4

This counterattack against White's Pawn position is considered premature. White gets a good lead in development and mobility by answering 5 B—N5.

BUDAPEST DEFENSE: 1 P—Q4, N—KB3; 2 P—QB4, P—K4

Black offers a Pawn in the hope of getting a strong attack. White generally gets the better game by playing for a lead in development; the extra Pawn is only of secondary importance.

CARO-KANN DEFENSE: 1 P—K4, P—QB3

A solid and phlegmatic defense which generally continues 2 P—Q4, P—Q4 without giving either side any marked winning possibilities.

CATALAN SYSTEM: 1 P—Q4, N—KB3; 2 P—QB4, P—K3; 3 N—KB3, P—Q4; 4 P—KN3

This line often transposes into the Reti Opening. White's fianchettoed Bishop at King Knight 2 frequently has great power. White thus gives Black the problem of neutralizing the power of the fianchettoed Bishop.

CENTER COUNTER GAME: 1 P—K4, P—Q4

After the usual continuation 2 PxP, QxP; 3 N—QB3 White drives away Black's Queen with loss of time for Black.

CENTER GAME: 1 P—K4, P—K4; 2 P—Q4, PxP; 3 QxP

Black gains a lasting lead in developing with 3 . . . N—QB3, attacking White's Queen. This is why the opening has practically disappeared from tournament play. (See Diagram 30.)

DANISH GAMBIT: 1 P—K4, P—K4; 2 P—Q4, PxP; 3 P—QB3

White offers a Pawn, and may offer a second one, for a lead in development. Whether or not he gets the attack he hopes for, depends on Black's resourcefulness and defensive skill.

DUTCH DEFENSE: 1 P—Q4, P—KB4

Black advances his King Bishop Pawn as a means of controlling the center. He holds in reserve the possibility of playing (a) . . . P—K3 and . . . P—Q4 or (b) . . . P—K3 and . . . P—Q3 or (c) . . . P—Q3 and . . . P—K4. Black has prospects of King-side attack, though White often has an opportunity to exploit Pawn weaknesses in Black's position.

ENGLISH OPENING: 1 P—QB4

White deliberately refrains from advancing a center Pawn, partly in order to wait until Black's intentions are revealed. This opening often transposes into the Reti Opening or Queen's Gambit Declined.

EVANS GAMBIT: 1 P—K4, P—K4; 2 N—KB3, N—QB3; 3 B—B4, B—B4; 4 P—QN4

This enterprising offshoot of the Giuoco Piano offers Black a Pawn in the hope of gaining time for a considerable lead in development and resulting attacking chances. Black's safest course is 4 . . . B—N3, seeking safety by refusing the Pawn. (See Diagram 18.)

FALKBEER COUNTER GAMBIT: 1 P—K4, P—K4; 2 P—KB4, P—Q4

This is a brisk method of declining the King's Gambit. It generally continues 3 KPxP, P—K5 when Black hopes to get enough compensation for the Pawn sacrificed. There are some brilliant games on record where inexact play by White allowed a fine finish by Black. But if White plays accurately and aggressively he should maintain the advantage.

FOUR KNIGHTS' GAME: 1 P—K4, P—K4; 2 N—KB3, N—QB3; 3 N—B3, N—B3

A safe but dull opening which is very likely to lead to a draw. There are many symmetrical variations where White's chances of initiative are reduced to a minimum. (See Diagram 15.)

FRENCH DEFENSE: 1 P—K4, P—K3

This is almost invariably continued 2 P—Q4, P—Q4 with a critical fight for control of the center. As a rule White has greater freedom of action, and Black is often hampered by the fact that his Queen Bishop has little mobility. However, the French is a serviceable defense that has some attractive counterattacking features. (See Diagram 44.)

GIUOCO PIANO: 1 P—K4, P—K4; 2 N—KB3, N—QB3; 3 B—B4, B—B4

This opening, the "Quiet Game," leads to unexciting chess when White later advances his Queen Pawn one square. But in those variations where White plays P—Q4, the resulting lines are generally very lively.

GRECO COUNTER GAMBIT: 1 P—K4, P—K4; 2 N—KB3, P—KB4

Black's counterattack against White's center is premature

and generally leaves White with a considerable lead in development.

GRUENFELD DEFENSE: 1 P—Q4, N—KB3; 2 P—QB4, P—KN3; 3 N—QB3, P—Q4

This is a "hypermodern" defense. Black is perfectly willing to let White set up a broad, formidable-looking Pawn center by 4 PxP, NxP; 5 P—K4 etc. In return, Black hopes to take pot-shots at this Pawn center by fianchettoing his King Bishop. Whether the Bishop's pressure on the center compensates for White's superior command of the board, is an open question.

HUNGARIAN DEFENSE: 1 P—K4, P—K4; 2 N—KB3, N—QB3; 3 B—B4, B—K2

Definitely a defense that favors White. Black's game is cramped and his development lacking in striking power. His reason for playing the defense is that he wishes to avoid the Giuoco Piano or the Evans Gambit.

KING'S GAMBIT: 1 P—K4, P—K4; 2 P—KB4, PxP

This is one of the oldest, liveliest, and most analyzed of all the chess openings. It has yielded White many flashy wins by quick attack along the King Bishop file. It has also resulted in snappy wins for Black when White's King was too exposed. Prudent players prefer to decline the gambit by 2 . . . B—B4. This leads to a more sedate tempo and gives Black an easier game without quite ruling out all the fireworks.

KING'S INDIAN DEFENSE: 1 P—Q4, N—KB3; 2 P—QB4, P—KN3 (followed by . . . P—Q3)

This defense leads to a very complex game with chances for both sides. It is one of the best fighting defenses in reply to 1 P—Q4. (See Diagrams 36, 56.)

NIMZOINDIAN DEFENSE: 1 P—Q4, N—KB3; 2 P—QB4, P—K3; 3 N—QB3, B—N5

Another great fighting defense. For the time being this leaves White in the dark as to whether Black will play . . . P—Q4, or . . . P—B4, or . . . P—Q3 followed by . . . P—K4. A possible drawback is that Black generally exchanges his advanced Bishop for White's Queen Knight. With the Bishop-pair at his disposal, White has promising attacking possibilities.

NIMZOVICH DEFENSE: 1 P—K4, N—QB3

A cramped, unpopular defense which offers Black poor prospects. White's strongest reply is 2 P—Q4.

PETROFF'S DEFENSE: 1 P—K4, P—K4; 2 N—KB3, N—KB3

Black can generally hold his own with this enterprising counterattack, despite the fact that Black's second move is attacking at an extremely early stage.

PHILIDOR'S DEFENSE: 1 P—K4, P—K4; 2 N—KB3, P—Q3

The early blocking of the King Bishop does Black no good. Black's pieces have little scope and the defense is therefore rarely played. (See Diagram 30.)

PONZIANI'S OPENING: 1 P—K4, P—K4; 2 N—KB3, N—QB3; 3 P—B3

White's third move is not aggressive enough and allows Black to counterattack comfortably with 3 . . . P—Q4! Since this counter menaces White's initiative, the opening is rarely seen in serious play. (See Diagram 41.)

QUEEN'S GAMBIT ACCEPTED: 1 P—Q4, P—Q4; 2 P—QB4, PxP

The acceptance of the gambit removes Black's Queen Pawn from the center and therefore often gives White a strong initiative based on his dominating position in the center. For this reason, Black generally declines the gambit. (See Diagram 32.)

QUEEN'S GAMBIT DECLINED: 1 P—Q4, P—Q4; 2 P—QB4, P—K3 (or 2 . . . P—QB3)

As indicated in the previous opening, Black declines the gambit in order to maintain a Pawn in the center. In this way he can fight for control of the center. In many variations, however, Black captures the gambit Pawn later in the game. There are two possible reasons for this. One is to begin simplifying exchanges which will free Black's game. The other reason is that this capture is often a prelude to a freeing maneuver based on . . . P—QB4 or . . . P—K4 or both.

This opening gives White many chances of exerting powerful pressure on Black's game. Thus, White is often in a position to exploit the hemmed-in position of Black's Queen Bishop. White's freedom of action is often decisive in other respects, too. Thus, he frequently makes winning use of an open Queen Bishop file, or a powerful outpost for a Knight at K5, or the powerful attacking diagonal QN1—KR7. (See Diagram 23.)

QUEEN'S INDIAN DEFENSE: 1 P—Q4, N—KB3; 2 P—QB4, P—K3; 3 N—KB3, P—QN3

This generally continues 4 P—KN3, B—N2; 5 B—N2 when we witness a duel between the two Bishops on the long diagonal. The opening favors White, who has a freer game. Black's chances of seizing the initiative are very slight.

RETI OPENING: 1 N—KB3, P—Q4; 2 P—B4

The "hypermodern" opening par excellence, dedicated to subtle maneuvering. White always fianchettoes the King Bishop and sometimes the other Bishop too. (For example: 2 . . . P—QB3; 3 P—QN3, N—B3; 4 P—N3, B—B4, 5 B—KN2 etc.) The resulting positions are usually suitable for slow-motion jockeying that would seriously tax the patience of the average player.

RUY LOPEZ: 1 P—K4, P—K4; 2 N—KB3, N—QB3; 3 B—N5

The powerful Bishop move puts Black's position under lasting pressure. This opening is considered the strongest, as far as White is concerned, of all those where both players advance the King Pawn two squares. If Black does not handle the opening carefully, he is likely to find himself in a seriously compromised position because of lack of terrain for his pieces.

SCOTCH GAME: 1 P—K4, P—K4; 2 N—KB3, N—QB3; 3 P—Q4, PxP; 4 NxP

This old-fashioned opening has lost much of the popularity it once enjoyed. By moving his King Knight twice, White wastes time and gives Black an opportunity to fight for the initiative with 4 . . . B—B4 or 4 . . . N—B3. The Scotch Gambit (4 B—QB4, B—B4) gives Black even less to worry about, and has altogether disappeared from serious play. (See Diagram 39.)

SICILIAN DEFENSE: 1 P—K4, P—QB4

The most courageous and the most aggressive of all the "irregular" replies to 1 P—K4. In all variations this defense leads to a complicated fighting game in which both players have chances for a win. This has always been the favorite defense of players who want lively play on ground of their own choosing. (See Diagram 35.)

THREE KNIGHTS' GAME: 1 P—K4, P—K4; 2 N—KB3, N—QB3; 3 N—B3, B—N5

Occasionally played to avoid the Four Knights' Game. It offers Black equality in a number of rather characterless variations.

TWO KNIGHTS' DEFENSE: 1 P—K4, P—K4; 2 N—KB3, N—QB3; 3 B—B4, N—B3

A lively opening, full of fight—especially if White tries to win the King Bishop Pawn with 4 N—N5. There are interesting variations, many of them complicated and some of them involving speculative Pawn sacrifices on both sides.

VIENNA GAME: 1 P—K4, P—K4; 2 N—QB3

Theoretically inferior to 2 N—KB3 as it does not attack Black's King Pawn and therefore gives Black time to develop and to try to seize the initiative. In playing this opening White generally aims at an early advance of his King Bishop Pawn, but theory gives Black even chances.

You will find this key useful in a number of ways. When you hear of an opening for the first time, you can consult the key to get an idea of what the opening is like. Again, by reading the description in the key, you can decide whether a given opening would suit your taste and style. By experimenting in this way, you will be able to decide on the openings you want to study and specialize in.

GLOSSARY

GLOSSARY

ATTACK: A move or series of moves with the intention or threat of checkmate or winning an advantage in material or position.

CASTLE: To play a special move with King and Rook that is possible only when the King has not moved previously in the game. To castle on the King-side involves moving the King to KN1 and the King Rook to KB1. In castling on the Queen-side, the King goes to QB1 and the Queen Rook to Q1.

CHECK: To attack the hostile King directly.

CHECKMATE: A check from which the King has no escape.

DEVELOPMENT: The process of bringing out the pieces from their original squares with a view to having them take an active part in the game.

DISCOVER CHECK: To move an intervening piece so that it exposes the hostile King to check by another hitherto screened piece.

DOUBLE CHECK: A discovered check which involves simultaneous check by the piece moving off the line of attack.

DRAWN GAME (or DRAW): A game which neither side wins. There is no winner, no loser.

EN PRISE: Subject to capture.

EXCHANGE: To capture a hostile piece for a piece of one's own. The units exchanged are *usually* of equivalent value—but not always. "THE EXCHANGE": A player is said to "win the Exchange" when he captures a Rook in return for a Bishop or Knight. To "lose the Exchange" is to give up a Rook in return for Bishop or Knight.

FIANCHETTO: Flank development of a Bishop to the KN2 or QN2 square.

FILES: The vertical rows of squares running up and down the board.

GAMBIT: An opening which involves the speculative offer of material.

PASSED PAWN: A pawn which is unopposed by hostile pawns on adjacent files.

PIN: An attack on a piece which is screening another piece from attack.

RANKS: The horizontal rows of squares running from side to side on the board.

RESIGN: To formally acknowledge defeat. This ends the game as if checkmate had taken place.

ROOK AND PAWN ENDING: An end-game in which only Kings, Rooks, and Pawns are left on the board.

SACRIFICE: To give up material for less valuable material of the enemy—with a view to achieving some object which is more important than the material sacrificed.

STALEMATE: A form of drawn game which results when the King, although not *in check*, is left only with moves that would put him in check.

TEMPO: A unit of time. (If a player takes two moves to do what he could have done in a single move, he is said to have lost a tempo.)

INDEX

Index